GAME, SHORE AND WATER

BIRDS OF INDIA

GAME, SHORE AND WATER

BIRDS OF INDIA.

COLONEL A. LE MESSURIER, R.E.

GYAN

Published by

GYAN

Gyan Publishing House
5, Ansari Road
Daryaganj, New Delhi-110002
Phone: 011-47034999, 9811692060
E-mail: books@gyanbooks.com

Distribution Network
gyanbooks.com
India, USA, Canada, UK, Australia, France

ISBN: 978-81-212-9274-0 (PB)
First Published, 1874

2nd Impression 2023

Printed at: Gyan Press, Delhi.

GAME, SHORE AND WATER BIRDS OF INDIA

AUTHOR: COLONEL A. LE MESSURIER

GAME, SHORE AND WATER

BIRDS OF INDIA.

BY

COLONEL A. LE MESSURIER, R.E.

ONE HUNDRED AND TWENTY-ONE ILLUSTRATIONS.

CALCUTTA:
THACKER, SPINK & CO., GOVERNMENT PLACE.
BOMBAY: THACKER & CO., LIMITED.
LONDON: W. THACKER & CO., 87 NEWGATE STREET.
1888.

PREFACE TO SECOND EDITION.

It was intended that an edition for the public should have been illustrated; but now that an expedition is starting for Central Asia, the Notes which were privately circulated in 1874 without the pictures are reprinted.

Some additions have been made, and the divisions into Families will now be found on pages 1, 9, and 22.

A. LE MESSURIER.

Simla, October 1878.

PREFACE TO FIRST EDITION.

(For Private Circulation only.)

To Sir William Merewether, C.B., K.C.S.I., Commissioner in Sind.

Dear Sir William,—

The accompanying Notes (commenced in 1861) on the Eastern Narra have been so often referred to by brother officers, that, after an interval of thirteen years, I have been induced to complete and print them, not only to satisfy inquiry, but to remove if possible the difficulty that exists in tracing Birds to their proper names.

The plan adopted is, it is hoped, both simple and concise. The Index shows the Birds in Classes, and these again are divided into Families on pages 1, 6, and 19, with references to the intermediate sheets on which the different species are detailed.

Errors and omissions must occur, and if at the close of the shooting-season those receiving copies will return them to me, I shall hope to complete my first intention of presenting them with others fully illustrated in exchange for their suggestions, corrections, and illustrations.

These may be "Dry Leaves" from an "Unhappy Valley," but they tell of the advantages that Sind offers to the sportsman in the abundance of its small game.

A. LE MESSURIER.

Kurrachee, November 1874.

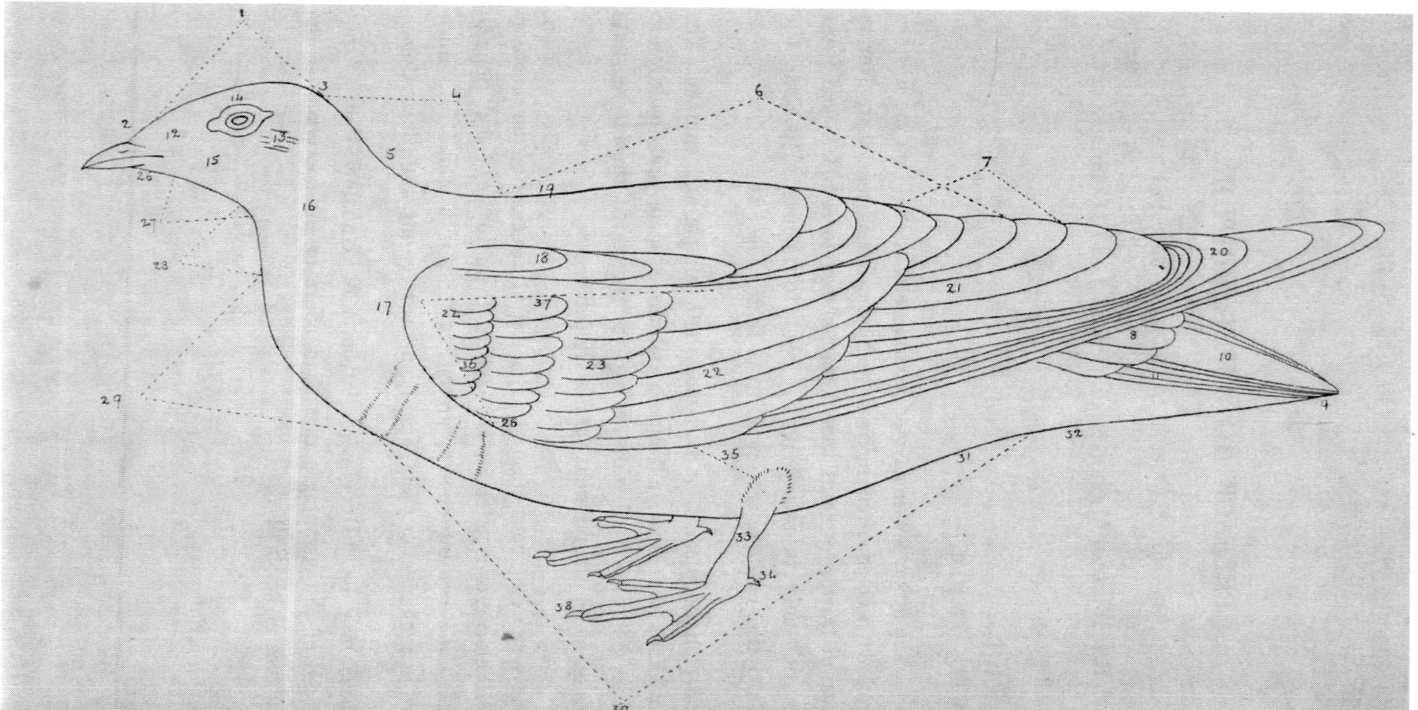

Diagram of 800. Painted Sand-Grouse (Hodgson).

References.

1. Crown (*Vertex*).
2. Forehead (*Frons*).
3. Hind head (*Occiput*).
4. Hind neck (*Cervix*).
5. Nape (*Nucha*).
6. Back (*Dorsum*).
7. Rump (*Uropygium*).
8. Upper Tail-coverts.
9. Tail-feathers (*Rectrices*).
10. Central Tail-feathers (*Uropygiales*).
11. Lateral or outer Tail-feathers.
12. Lore.
13. Ear-coverts (*Regio parotica*).
14. Eyebrow (*Supercilium*).
15. Cheek.
16. Side of Neck (*Collum*).
17. Shoulder (*Humerus*).
18. Scapulars or Humerals (*Parapteron*).
19. Interscapulary region (*Interscapulium*).
20. Primaries or Metacarpo-digitals } (*Remiges*).
21. Secondaries or Cubitals }
22. Greater coverts }
23. Middle coverts } (*Tectrices*).
24. Lesser coverts }
25. Winglet or Bastard Wing (*Ala spuria* or *Alula*).
26. Chin (*Mentum*).
27. Throat (*Gula*).
28. Fore neck (*Jugulum*).
29. Breast (*Pectus*).
30. Abdomen.
31. Vent (*Crissum*).
32. Under Tail-coverts.
33. Tarsus.
34. First or Hind Toe (*Hallux*).
35. Tibia.
36. Carpus.
37. Radius and Ulna.
38. Digit or Toe.

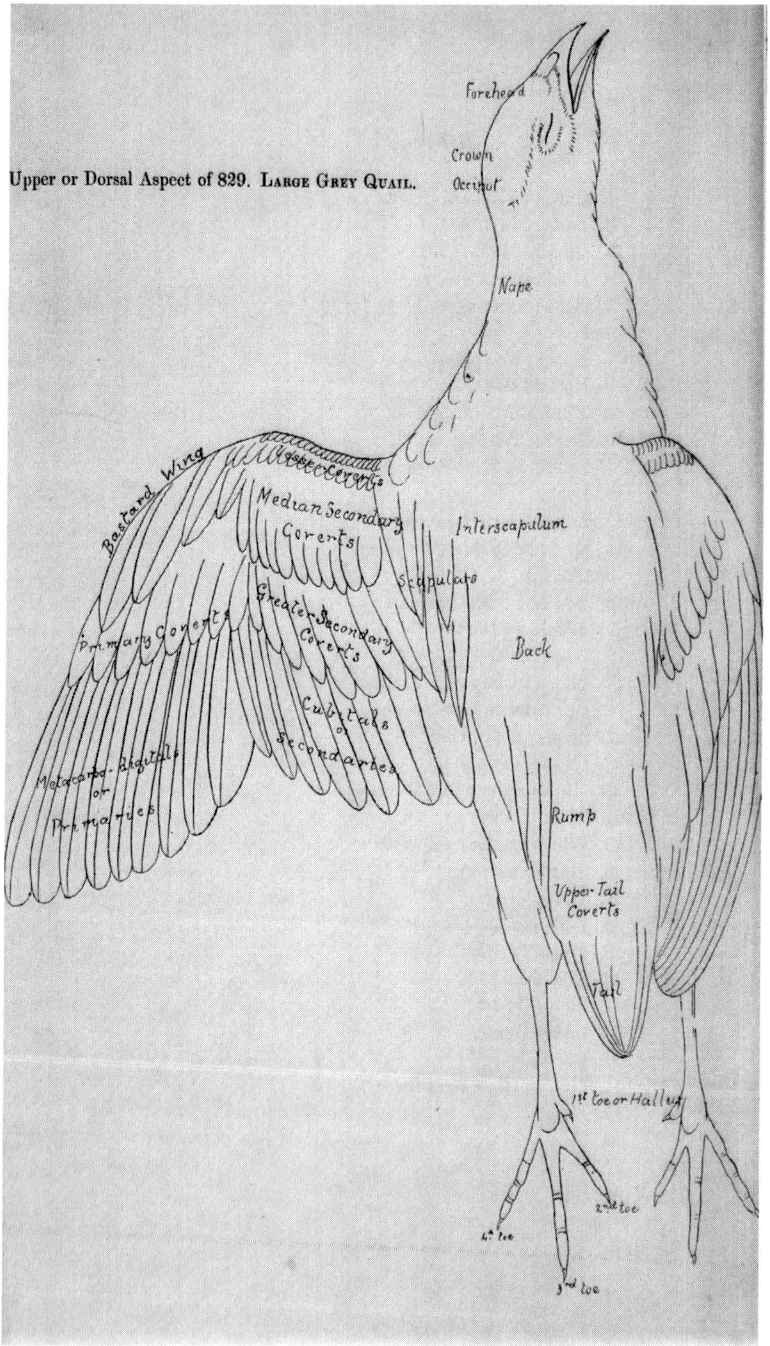

Upper or Dorsal Aspect of 829. LARGE GREY QUAIL.

Under or Ventral Aspect of 870. PINTAIL SNIPE (Hodgson).

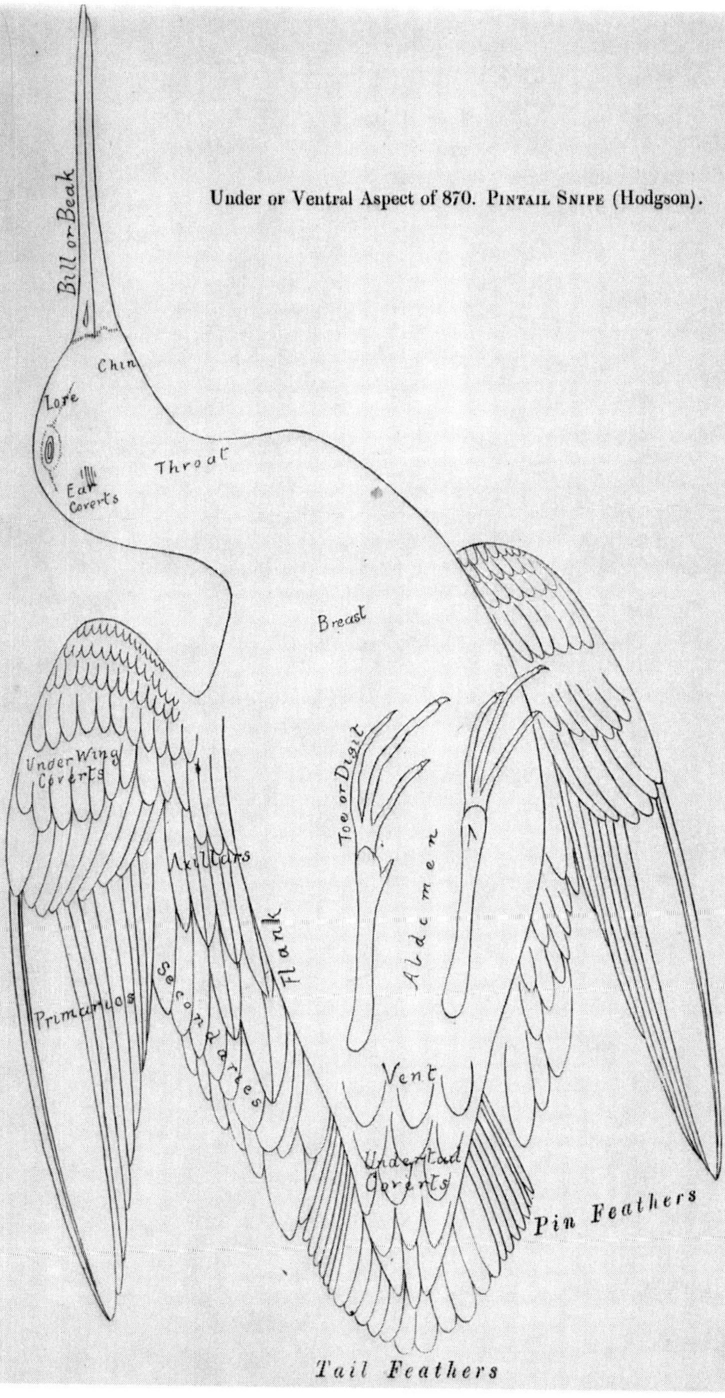

The Exo-Skeleton, or Feathers.

The Remiges, or Flight-Feathers.

The feathers of a wing of a bird have a very definite arrangement. They consist of the large quill-feathers (*Remiges*, or flight-feathers) and the coverts (*Tectrices*).

The *Remiges* are developed into the wing-membrane (*ala membrana*), and come into close and definite relation to the bones, forming two well-marked groups:—

(i.) The cubitals, or "secondaries," are attached to the ulna, and vary greatly in number in different groups of birds.

(ii.) The metacarpo-digitals, or "primaries," are attached to the bones of the manus, and are typically eleven in number. Of these the metacarpus bears six (the "metacarpals"), and the phalanges of the digits bear five (the "digitals"), disposed as follows:—One (the "addigital") lying upon the phalanx of digit iii., and inserted at the metacarpo-phalangeal articulation; two (the "middigitals") inserted on the first phalanx of digit ii.; and two (the "predigitals") inserted on the second phalanx of digit ii. The most distal of these (the "remicle") is always rudimentary, and sometimes absent. The bones of digit i. always bear a small number of more or less developed quill-feathers, forming the "bastard wing" (*ala spuria* or *alula*).

In many birds there is a development of large feathers lying over the distal half of the humerus, resembling remiges, but really continuous with the series of greater coverts; these are called "humerals" (*Parapteron*). Corresponding with these on the surface of the wing are the "axillaries" (*Hypopteron*).

The Arrangement of the Coverts.

The coverts of the upper surface of the wing (*Tectrices superiores*) are divided into *Tectrices majores*, *T. mediæ*, and *T. minores*. Those of the lower surface are *Tectrices inferiores*. The relative development of these series of coverts varies much in different groups of birds.

The most important, or "Principal Coverts," are the *Tectrices majores*, consisting of one row of upper coverts attached to the bases of the remiges, and a row of inferior coverts attached in a similar way. Each remex has thus two principal coverts in relation to it, one on its upper or dorsal, and one on its lower or ventral surface.

The dorsal covert of the first metacarpal remex is generally rudimentary, in compliance with mechanical requirements in the folding of the wing.

Modifications of the Cubital or Secondary Remiges.

Beyond variation in number and form, the only important modification in this series consists in the absence in many birds (Owls, Eagles, Geese, Pigeons, Grebes, &c.) of the fifth remex (counting from the carpal joint), the coverts being retained. This condition is "Aquin cubitalism;" when the feather is present the condition is called "Quin cubitalism."

Modifications of the Metacarpo-digital or Primary Remiges.

The typical condition of the metacarpo-digital remiges being as described above, the following are the principal modifications:—

I. The metacarpals may be increased to seven (as in Grebes, Flamingoes, and Storks).

II. A decrease in the number of digitals may take place at distal end of wing.

(*a*) A remicle may be lost, its principal coverts being retained (as in Turkey, Goose, &c.).

(*b*) The remicle and its coverts may disappear, and, in addition, the next predigital (2) may disappear also (as in "nine-primaried birds"), though generally some trace of it may be found. Among *Passeres* almost every gradation in the development of these feathers may be met with. (Nat. Hist. Museum.)

The Bill or Beak of Birds consists of two parts, generally called the upper and lower mandibles, but more properly *maxilla* and *mandible.*

The externally visible part of each is an epidermic sheath of horny, or sometimes leathery, consistence, which covers the anterior bony prolongation of the cranium in the one case (the *premaxillary* bone), and of the lower jaw in the other (the *dentary* bone).

In most birds the sheath (*rhamphotheca*) of each jaw is entire, but in some (as the Petrels) it is "pieced" or divided into distinct parts by various lines of slight connection.

The different parts of the bill have received names useful for descriptive purposes. Of these the following are the most important:—

The whole length of the middle line of the upper surface, from the tip or apex to where the feathers commence on the forehead, is called the *culmen.*

The lateral sharp edge of the horny covering of either maxilla or mandible is the *tomium.*

The point at which the edges of the jaws meet behind is the *commissure,* or *angle* of the mouth (sometimes called the *gape*).

The mandible is composed of two lateral halves, called *rami* or branches, separate behind, but united in front; the space between them where they are separate is the *inter-ramal space*; the lower median edge of the mandible, from the point at which the *rami* unite to the tip, is called the *gonys*.

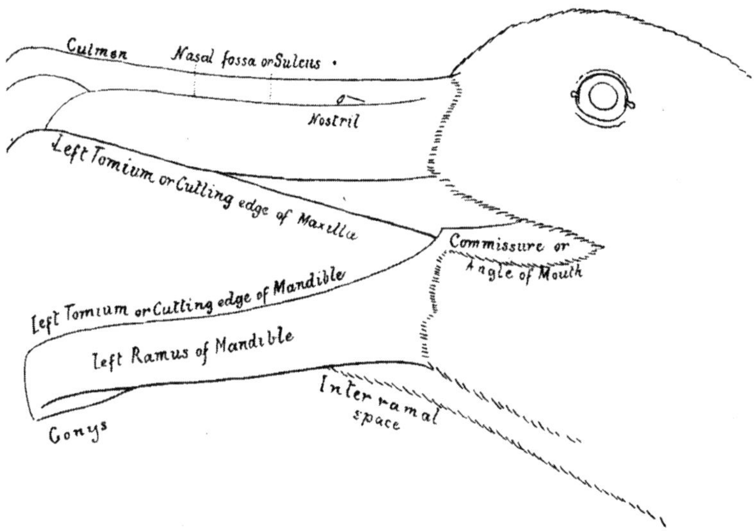

Nat. Hist. Museum.

The nostrils are two in number, situated usually near the base of the maxilla. Their form and exact position vary considerably in different birds. They often open into a depression or groove (the *nasal fossa* or *sulcus*). In the Petrels (*Tubinares*) the borders of the nostrils are prolonged forwards in a tubular form. In some birds (as Hawks and Parrots) they open in a soft waxy-looking covering of the base of the maxilla, called the *cere*. In the *Apteryx* alone of existing birds the nostrils open near the tip of the bill. (Nat. Hist. Museum.)

Posterior Extremity, or Leg, of Birds.

The hind limb consists of three principal divisions:—

I. The thigh, or *femur*. II. The leg, or *crus*. III. The foot, or *pes*. The latter has a more or less undivided portion, called, in ornithological language, the *tarsus*, but the skeleton of which corresponds to the united three metatarsal bones of mammals, to which is also joined the lower or distal part of the tarsus proper. The other portion of the true tarsus is united to the lower end of the tibia. The ankle-joint is therefore not situated between the tibia and tarsus, as in mammals, but in the middle of the tarsus itself.

To the lower end of the tarso-metatarsal bone the three principal (second, third, and fourth) digits, or toes, are attached. The first digit has a separate, or accessory, metatarsal bone, of which only the lower end is developed, and which is usually attached loosely to the hinder surface of the principal bone.

The front, or dorsal, surface of the tarsus is called the *acrotarsium*, the back the *planta*, as it corresponds to the sole of the foot of man and plantigrade animals. (Nat. Hist. Museum.)

Number of the Digits, or Toes.

Birds have usually four toes, never more; in some cases only three; in the Ostrich alone two. These are designated the first, second, third, and fourth. The one attached to the accessory metatarsal bone, and which is almost always directed backwards, being called the first or

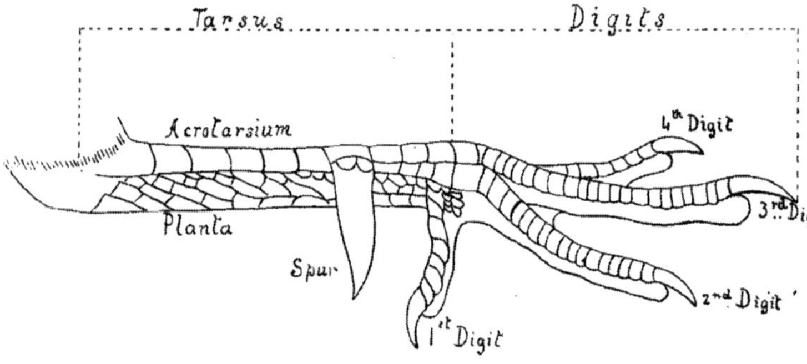

812. Red Jungle-Fowl (Gray).

hallux. The second toe has normally three phalanges; it is the inner one of these that turns forwards. The third has four phalanges, and it is the middle toe of these that is usually directed forwards. The fourth has five phalanges, and is the outer toe.

Reduction from the normal number of Toes.

When one of the four normal toes is absent it is almost always the first, or hallux, which may be entirely suppressed or exist in a rudimentary condition, the bones being present but concealed beneath the skin.

It is not always the hallux which is absent in three-toed birds. In the Kingfishers of the genera *Ceyx* and *Alcyone* the hallux is well developed; but the second digit is reduced to its basal phalanx, appearing externally merely as a wart-like eminence.

In the Passerine genus *Cholornis* the fourth, or external, digit is in a rudimentary condition.

In the Ostrich two digits only are present, which represent the third and fourth of the normal foot. The small size of the latter, and the frequent absence of its nail, indicate a tendency to reduction to a single toe (the third), as in the Horse among Mammals.

Position of the Toes.

The vast majority of birds have three toes in front and one (the hallux, or first toe) behind.

Exceptions:—

1. All four toes may be turned forwards, as in the *Coliidæ* and some Swifts (*Cypselidæ*).

2. The first toe may be versatile, turning backwards or forwards.

3. The outer front toe (fourth) may be versatile, or capable of being turned backwards or forwards, as in most Owls and the Osprey (*Pandion*).

4. The toes may be permanently in pairs, two before and two behind, as in Woodpeckers, Toucans, Cuckoos, and others, a condition described as *Zygodactyle*, or yoke-toed. In these cases it is always the first and fourth that turn backward, except in the Trogons, where it is the first and second. The third toe is invariably directed forwards. (Nat. Hist. Museum.)

Leading Modifications of the Foot of Birds.

There are three functional plans or types upon which birds' feet are constructed, each with various modifications and with transitional forms connecting them.

I. The Perching or Insessorial type, in which the foot is best fitted for the grasping function required in perching on trees.

(*a*) The typical *Passerine* modification.—All the toes free and movable, and the hinder one well developed; the foot is thus like a hand with three fingers and an opposite thumb. *Examples*: Song-Thrush (*Turdus musicus*) and Sky-Lark (*Alauda arvensis*).

(*b*) The *Raptorial* modification.—The toes armed with powerful curved sharp claws and widely spread, so that they may have greater power in seizing and holding their prey. Their under surface bulbous, scabrous, or even spiny, for greater security in grasping. *Examples*: Osprey (*Pandion haliaëtus*) and Sea-Eagle (*Haliaëtus albicilla*).

(*c*) The *Syndactyle* modification, in which the outer and middle toes are coherent for most of their extent, with a broad sole in common. This occurs in perching birds, as Kingfishers, which scarcely use their feet for progression, but simply for sitting motionless. *Examples*: Kingfisher (*Ceryle torquatus*), Hornbill (*Buceros rhinoceros*), Cock of the Rock (*Rupicola crocea*).

(*d*) The *Zygodactyle*, or yoke-toed modification.—Two toes are turned forwards and two backwards. This occurs in many families of birds not otherwise related either in structure or habits. *Examples*: Wryneck (*Yunx torquilla*), Common Cuckoo (*Cuculus canorus*), Indian Koel (*Eudynamys honorata*), Red-and-Blue Macaw (*Ara macao*).

II. The Walking or Wading (*Cursorial* or *Grallatorial*) type.—In this form the foot has the grasping power, but is especially adapted for walking on the ground. The hind toe is elevated above the level of the others, and reduced in size or totally lost. In some wading birds the intervals between the toes are completely or partially webbed. *Examples*: Pheasant (*Phasianus colchicus*), Heron (*Ardea cinerea*), Pheasant-tailed Jacana (*Hydrophasianus chirurgus*), Moorhen (*Gallinula chloropus*), Red-necked Avocet (*Recurvirostra avocetta*).

III. The Swimming or Natatorial type.—By the development of webs between the toes the foot is transformed into a swimming instrument, usually with much loss of its power of perching and running.

(*a*) The *Lobate* modification.—The toes not united together by webs but furnished with lobes or flaps along the sides, as in the Coot (*Fulica atra*) and Crested Grebe (*Podiceps cristatus*).

(*b*) The ordinary *Palmate* modification.—All the front toes united by webs. The hind toe free, as in the Wild Duck (*Anas boschas*), Black-headed Gull (*Larus ridibundus*), Skimmer (*Rhynchops flavirostris*).

(*c*) The *Totipalmate* modification.—Webs not only between the front toes, but also extending between the second and first, or hind toe; so that all four are united together, as in the Pelican (*Pelecanus onocrotalus*). (Nat. Hist. Museum.)

RASORES.

GAME BIRDS.

Order.	Suborder.	Family.
RASORES. (SCRATCHERS.) *GAME BIRDS.* (Type, Domestic Fowl.) Bill strong, short, arched. Wings usually short and rounded. Legs very stout. Feet formed for walking.	Hind toe on same plane as anterior ones	**CRACIDÆ.**—No spurs. Toes long an toe long. Tail of 14 feathers ...... **MEGAPODIDÆ.**—Large strong feet Tail of 12 feathers, not always de toe long. Plumage dull green-brow a fowl. Frequent sandy soil ......
	Hind toe raised above level of others or wanting	**PTEROCLIDÆ.**—Tarsus feathered i long and pointed. Hind toe very Orbits more or less nude. Plum variegated with brown. Tail of 16 rapid. Feed on seeds .... **PHASIANIDÆ.**—Head often furnish nude skin, or lappets and wattles. feathers, much developed. Tarsus in males. Hind toe raised. Freq thick cover. Roost on trees ...... **TETRAONIDÆ.**—Wings rounded i tail very short. Hind toe elevated. Differ slightly in sexes. Frequen jungle .... **TURNICIDÆ.**—Bill slender. Wing short or none. Lateral toes short. toe small or none. Frequent b jungle .... **CHIONIDIDÆ** .... **TINAMIDÆ** ....

* Not repr

	Subfamily.	Genus.	Page.
lender. Hind	PENELOPINÆ	GUANS *	6
	CRACINÆ	CURASSOWS *	6
d large claws. oped. Hind Smaller than	TALEGALLINÆ	TALEGALLAS *	6
	MEGAPODINÆ	MOUND-BIRDS	6
ront. Wings hort or none. pale yellow, hers. Flight	....	ROCK- or SAND-GROUSE	7
with crests or il of 18 to 20 ually spurred t forests and	PAVONINÆ	PEAFOWLS	11
		PEA-PHEASANTS	11
	PHASIANINÆ	MOONALS	13
		TRAGOPANS	14
		BLOOD-PHEASANTS	15
		CHEER (TRUE) PHEASANTS	16
		KALIJ PHEASANTS	16
		SILVER PHEASANTS	17
		FIREBACKS	18
	GALLINÆ	JUNGLE-FOWLS	18
		SPUR-FOWLS	19
	MELEAGRINÆ	TURKEYS *	20
		GUINEA-FOWLS *	20
ost. Bill and lumage game. rass and low	PERDICINÆ	SNOW-COCKS	20
		SNOW-PARTRIDGES	21
		PARTRIDGES	21
		WOOD-PARTRIDGES	25
		JUNGLE-QUAILS	28
	COTURNICINÆ	TRUE QUAILS	29
	ODONTOPHORINÆ	AMERICAN PARTRIDGES *	31
	TETRAONINÆ	TRUE GROUSE *	31
oderate. Tail spurs. Hind s and grass-	TURNICINÆ	BUSTARD QUAILS	32
		BUTTON-QUAILS	32
....	CHIONIDINÆ	SHEATHBILLS *	34
....	TINAMINÆ	TINAMOUS *	34

ted in India.

Order **RASORES.** *GAME BIRDS.*

Scratchers. Type, Domestic Fowl.

Gallinaceous (or Game) Birds, of which the Domestic Fowl may be taken as a type, are termed Rasores (*Rado, ĕre, rasi, rasum,* to scratch up), from their habit of scratching in the ground for grain, seeds, roots, and insects as food. They do not wash in water, but flutter in the dust, and almost all nestle on the ground. Many are polygamous, and in these the male bird is the larger and adorned with a much richer plumage. The female is prolific; the young are born covered with down, and run as soon as hatched.

This order is remarkable in comprising so many species capable of domestication, in having the tarsal spur (considered as representing the thumb), in the presence, in most of the groups, of the accessory plume to the clothing-feathers, and in the bastard secondary feather of the wing. Owing to the simple construction of the windpipe and muscles they cannot modulate the voice.

Game Birds evince many interesting analogies with ruminating animals among Mammals. The crop may be said to represent the paunch, and the cœca of both are large. They both have a low degree of intelligence, are easily domesticated, and are more prone to variation than most other tribes. The head, too, is, in many of both orders, adorned with appendages, horns, and crests, and they afford more wholesome food to man than any other orders.

Game Birds are found over the greater part of the world, but the finest groups and greatest variety of form are from Asia.

Bill strong, short, arched. Wings usually short and rounded. Legs very stout. Feet formed for walking.

A. *Hind toe on same plane as anterior ones.*

Family CRACIDÆ. GUANS and CURASSOWS.

No spurs. Toes long and slender. Hind toe long. Tail of 14 feathers.

Exclusively American. By their habits they appear to be the link that joins the Pigeons to the Game Birds. There are three genera of Guans:—1. *Ortalida,* from warmer parts of S. America; 2. *Penelope*; 3. *Oreophasis,* from Guatemala; and two genera of Curassows:—1. *Crax,* from Tropical America, and 2. *Pauxi.*

Family MEGAPODIDÆ. MOUND-BIRDS.

Large strong feet and large claws. Tail of 12 feathers, not always developed. Hind toe long. Plumage dull green-brown. Smaller than a Fowl. Frequent sandy soil.

Mound-Birds are distributed as under:—1. *Megapodius* in N.W. Australia and Eastern Archipelago. 2. *Leipoa* (the Australian Pheasant) in S.W. Australia. 3. *Mesites* in Madagascar. Jerdon thinks that the Lyre-bird of Australia (*Menura superba*) is more nearly allied to the Megapodes than to the Wrens and Warblers.

Subfamily TALEGALLINÆ. TALEGALLAS.

The Talegallas include *T. lathami,* the Brush-Turkey of Australia, *T. cuvieri* from New Guinea, and *M. maleo* from the island of Celebes.

Subfamily MEGAPODINÆ.

Large strong feet, placed far back.

Genus **MEGAPODIUS.**

μέγας = great; πούς = a foot.

Dull green plumage. Long hind toe. Tail of 12 feathers.

Megapodius nicobariensis. THE NICOBAR MEGAPODE.

♂ $14\frac{1}{2}''$ to $17''$; $1\frac{1}{4}$ to $2\frac{1}{8}$ lbs. Legs dark horny. Bill greenish. Orbits brick-red. Crown pale olive, grey behind ears. Above olive-brown, below grey-brown. Breast tinged grey.—*Young* snuff-brown, with tail like bunch of fur. ('Stray Feathers,' ii. 276.)

B. *Hind toe raised above level of others or wanting.*

Family PTEROCLIDÆ. SAND-GROUSE.

Found in Southern Europe, Africa, and Asia. Placed by Jerdon as a distinct natural family. Gray groups them as a subfamily of Tetraonidæ, with which they only agree in having feathered tarsus.

Tarsus feathered in front. Wings long and pointed. Hind toe very short or none. Orbits more or less nude. Plumage pale yellow, variegated with brown. Tail of 16 feathers. Flight rapid. Feed on seeds.

Genus **PTEROCLES.**

πτερόν = a feather; *κλείς* = a bar.

Male uniformly coloured.—*Female* more or less spotted or barred. First and second quills longest. Toes bare. Minute hind toe raised.

(i.) *With tail-feathers graduated.*

799. Pterocles arenarius. THE LARGE OR BLACK-BELLIED SAND-GROUSE.

Ărēnārius = pertaining to sand, *arēna*.

Bhut-titur, Buk-tit, *Upper India*; **Banchur,** *Peshawar*; **Siahsin** (Persian), *Khorassan*; **Bagrikara** (Turkish), *N. Persia.*

Jerome-Khojak, 1879.

♂ 13¼″ to 14¾″; 18 oz. ♀ 13″ to 14″. Legs dull yellow. Bill bluish. Central tail-feathers slightly lengthened. Primaries slate, with black shafts. Abdomen and breast-band black.—*Male* above mottled ashy and fulvous. Orange wing-band. Chin deep chestnut. Black triangle on throat. Breast fawn.—*Female*: Breast, head, and above fulvous, banded brown. Chin fulvous, with black edges and specks.

800. Pterocles fasciatus. THE PAINTED SAND-GROUSE.

Fascio (no perf.), *atum* = to swathe or envelop in bands.
Bhut-titur, Bhut-bur, *N. W. P.*; **Palki,** *Belgaum*; **Handeri,** *S. India*; **Pokundi** (Marathi); **Kal gowjal haki** (Kanarese), *Mysore*; **Sonda polanka** (Telugu).

♂ $10\frac{1}{2}''$ to $11\frac{1}{4}''$; 6 to $7\frac{1}{2}$ oz. ♀ $10''$ to $10\frac{1}{2}''$. Legs dull yellow. Bill red. Primaries brown-black, with pale edgings. Abdomen black, with crescentic white marks.—*Male* above yellow, banded brown. Four stripes on forehead. Triple breast-band. Wing-coverts banded black, edged white.—*Female*: Breast and above finely barred. Abdomen finely barred, chocolate and cream-white.

Pterocles lichtensteini. THE CLOSE-BARRED SAND-GROUSE.

In honour of Lichtenstein.

♂ $10\frac{3}{4}''$; 8 oz. ♀ $10\frac{1}{3}''$. Legs orange. Bill flesh-brown. Primaries hair-brown, margined dull white. Resembles *P. fasciatus*. Abdomen white, with crescentic black marks. Neck-feathers yellowish white, tipped black spot.—*Female*: Chin, throat albescent, closely speckled blackish brown. (S. F. i. 219.)

Pterocles coronatus. THE CORONETTED SAND-GROUSE.

Cŏrōno, avi, atum = to crown, wreathe.
Katinga, *Sind.*

♂ $10\frac{1}{2}''$ to $11\frac{1}{2}''$; 8 oz. ♀ $10''$ to $10\frac{1}{2}''$. Legs fawn. Bill bluish. Primaries umber, white shafts, some with inner webs edged rufous. Yellow cheek-patch.—*Male*: Black stripe on each side of the bill, and one from chin down throat. Above light brown, mixed grey.—*Female*: Brown pale cinnamon, spotted black. Neck, breast, and above cinnamon, barred dusky. Abdomen fawn, faintly speckled.

(ii.) *With medial tail-feathers greatly elongated.*

801. Pterocles alchata. LARGE PINTAIL or SOLITARY SAND-GROUSE.

♂ $14''$ to $15\frac{1}{2}''$; 10 to 12 oz. ♀ $13\frac{1}{2}''$ to $15''$; 8 to $11\frac{1}{4}$ oz. Legs plumbeous. Bill brown. Primaries slate, inner webs brown. Median tail blackish.—*Male*: Stripe behind eye. Bands on crown and nape. Chin, throat, and double breast-band black. Above olive-grey. Abdomen white.—*Female*: Throat white, with half-collar black. Above barred black, with ashy spots.

Supposed Quail of the Israelites.

802. Pterocles exustus. THE COMMON or ROCK SAND-GROUSE.

Exuro, ussi, ustum = to burn up.

Bur-titur, Kuhar, *N. W. P.*; **Batiban,** *Sind*; **Popandi** (Bheel); **Pokandi,** *Deccan*; **Palki,** *Belgaum*; **Jam-polanka** (Telugu); **Kal-Kondari** (Tamil).

♂ $11\frac{3}{4}''$ to $13\frac{3}{4}''$; 8 to 10 oz. ♀ $11''$ to $12\frac{1}{4}''$; $7\frac{1}{2}$ to $8\frac{1}{3}$ oz. Legs plumbeous. Bill plumbeous. Primaries black, tips, except of first four, white. Plain bar on wing.—*Male* above dusty green. Abdomen

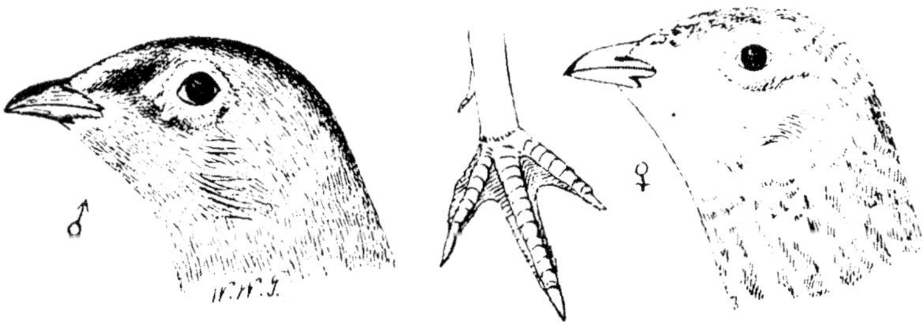

Dorbajee, 8-8-72.

chocolate. Narrow black breast-band.—*Female*: Abdomen chocolate, closely barred. Neck and breast spotted. Above fulvous, barred brown. —*Young* have mixed plumage alternately edged and barred.

Pterocles senegalus. THE SPOTTED SAND-GROUSE.

Gutu, *Sind.*

♂ $13\frac{1}{2}''$ to $11\frac{2}{3}''$; 9 to 12 oz. ♀ $11''$ to $12\frac{1}{4}''$; 8 to 9 oz. Legs blue-grey. Bill plumbeous, dark tip. Primaries pale madder-brown, black shafts, first three tipped black, rest tipped white. Chin and throat-patch yellow. Abdominal line sooty.—*Male*: Crown and nape dove-colour. Neck, breast, and eye-patch ash-grey. Above fulvous yellow. —*Female*: Neck and above dotted dusky grey on buff.

Genus **SYRRHAPTES.**

Syrrhaptes derived by Illiger from *συῤῥάπτειν* = to sew or stitch together, because the last phalanges of the toes alone are free.

No hind toe. Feathered to claws. First and second quills lengthened; second quill longest.

Syrrhaptes tibetanus. THE THIBETAN SAND-GROUSE.

Kaling, Kuk, *Ladak.*

♂ 18″ to 20″. ♀ 16½″ to 18″. Bill bluish. Legs feathered to the claws. Primaries black, with white patch on inner web of hinder ones. —*Male*: Crown and nape white, closely barred. Narrow yellow band across back of neck. Black blotches on inner web of scapulars. Breast grey. Abdomen white.—*Female*: whole breast lineated with zigzag brown lines. ('Lahore to Yarkand,' p. 259.)

"*Baguerlac*," the *Tetra paradoxus* of Pallas, known as *S. pallasi*, is Marco's bird (Yule's 'Marco Polo,' p. 240).

Tĕtrăo = *τετράων*, a bird mentioned by Athenæus and Pliny. *Paradoxus* = *παράδοξος*, strange, contrary to expectation; from the curious structure of its feet.

Family PHASIANIDÆ.

Head often furnished with crests or nude skin, or lappets and wattles. Tail of 18 to 20 feathers, much developed. Tarsus usually spurred in males. Hind toe raised. Frequent forests and thick cover. Roost on trees.

Subfamily PAVONINÆ. PEAFOWL and PEA-PHEASANTS.

Plumage more or less ocellated. Inhabit Thibet, India (not extending into Himalayas), Burmah, and some of the islands of the Indian Ocean.

Genus **PAVO.**

Pavo = proper name = Peacock; the same as Greek *ταῶς*, Anglo-Saxon *pawa*, English *Peafowl.*

Tail of 18 feathers. One spur. Long upper tail-coverts beautifully ocellated.

803. Pavo cristatus. THE COMMON PEAFOWL.

Mor, *India*; **Mujur,** *Terai*; **Myl** (Tamil); **Nimili** (Telugu); **Nowl** (Canarese), *Mysore.*

♂ 42″ to 48″ to end of true tail, train 40″ to 48″; 9 to 11¼ lbs. ♀ 36″ to 40″, train 12″ to 15″; 6 to 8½ lbs. Legs grey-brown. Bill horny brown. Crest of 24 feathers webbed at tips. Head, neck, and breast purple. Above green. Primaries and tail chestnut. Train green. Abdomen black.—*Female*: Head and neck chestnut. Above light brown, with faint wavings. Tail light brown, tips white.

Pavo muticus. THE BURMESE PEAFOWL.

Doun, Doung (Burmese).

♂ 40″ to 48″, train 24″ to 44″; 8½ to 11 lbs. Legs horny brown. Bill greyish. Long crest of 10 or more feathers regularly barbed from base. Blue crown. White eye and cheek-patch fringed beneath with chrome-yellow. Lesser wing-coverts, tertiaries, and their coverts and scapulars of uniform colour and unbarred. (H. & M. i. 93.)

Genus **POLYPLECTRUM.**

πολὺς = many, *πλῆκτρον* = an instrument to strike with, a quill.

Tail of 16 feathers. Males beautifully adorned all over with green or pink ocelli. Two or three spurs.

Polyplectrum tibetanum. THE GREY PEA-PHEASANT.

Doungkulla, *Arakan and Pegu*; **Munnowar,** *Assam*; **Deadurug,** *Garo Hills.*

♂ 24½″ to 26″, tail 12½″ to 14″; 1½ to 1¾ lbs. ♀ 19″, tail 8″; 14 oz. to 1 lb. Legs plumbeous. Bill horny brown. Spots grey-white on grey-brown ground. White chin. Facial skin pale yellow. Crest brush-like. Large green ocelli on tail.—*Female*: Head and neck dark brown, finely barred. Primaries and greater coverts liver-brown. Back, rump, and upper tail-coverts minutely pencilled buff-brown. Breast and abdomen hair-brown, minutely speckled. (S. F. i. 36; H. & M. i. 110.)

Polyplectrum bicalcaratum. THE MALAYAN PEA-PHEASANT.

Calcar, aris = a spur.
Quon-chermin (Malay).

♂ 20½″. ♀ 18″. Legs dusk. Bill blackish. Spots hair-brown on buff ground. Orbital space red. (S. F. i. 36; H. & M. i. 114.)

Polyplectrum germaini. THE LOOSHAI PEA-PHEASANT.

General colour black-brown, irregularly spotted light brown. Head, back of neck black, each feather barred white. Back, wing, and tail-coverts with metallic spots, lustrous green and rich purple. Primaries dark brown. Bill black. Feet black. (S. F. vii. 426.)

Genus ARGUS.

Argus, King of Argos, had 100 eyes, of which two only were asleep at one time. Juno put the eyes of Argus on the tail of the Peacock, a bird sacred to her divinity.

Tail of 12 feathers. Secondaries longer than primaries. Covered with fine ocelli. No spur.

Argus giganteus. THE ARGUS PEA-PHEASANT.

Quon (Malay); **Kyek-wah,** *Siam.*

♂ 70″ to 73″, tail from vent 49″ to 52″; 4½ to 5½ lbs. ♀ 27″ to 30″, tail from vent 12½″ to 13″; 3¼ to 3¾ lbs. Legs bright red. Bill white.

Remarkable for its beauty. The wings painted and ocellated beyond description. Secondaries three times as large as primaries. Facial skin dull pale indigo. This is the Chinese Pheasant.

Genus CROSSOPTILON.

κροσσὺς = shaggy hair, a tuft of hair; πτίλον = a feather.

Crossoptilon tibetanum. HODGSON'S EARED PHEASANT.

♂ 38″ to 40″, tail 19″ to 20″. Legs bright red. Bill dull red. Eye-patch and cheek red. Crest-feathers black, short, erect, velvety, and thick-set. Sixth quill longest. 18 tail-feathers, satin-green or black. Neck, back, and abdomen yellowish grey-white.

Subfamily PHASIANINÆ. PHEASANTS.

In which Jerdon includes Moonals, Tragopans, Blood, Pucras, Cheer, Fireback, Kalij, and Silver Pheasants. They inhabit Asia, Himalayas, India, Japan, and China, and do not (excepting some of the Kalij group) extend into Burmah and not at all into Malayana.

Plumage rarely ocellated. Central tail-feathers sometimes very long. Head more or less crested. Tail, in most, of 18 feathers.

Genus **LOPHOPHORUS.**

λόφος = a crest; φορέω = I carry.

Crest-feathers lanceolate at tip.—*Male*: One short spur. Plumage metallic green and gold. Rufous tail of 16 feathers.

804. Lophophorus impeyanus. THE MOONAL PHEASANT.

Nil-mor, *Kashmir*; **Moonal,** *Himalayas*; **Datteya,** *Thibet*; **Dangan,** *Nepal*; **Chamdong,** *Sikkim.*

♂ 26″ to 29″; 4½ to 5¼ lbs. ♀ 24″ to 26″; 4 to 5 lbs. Legs ashy green. Bill dark horny.—*Male*: Head and throat metallic green. Above glossed purple and green. Middle of back white.—*Female* pale brown, with dark spots and bars. Chin and throat white.—*Young* in first year resemble females, with chin, throat, and vent spotted black. Males in second year spotted all over with glossy green. Seventh quill retains brown till third year.

Lophophorus sclateri. THE CRESTLESS MOONAL PHEASANT.

♂ 27″. Legs dark brown. Bill yellowish. Bright blue eye-patch. Entire lower parts and wing-lining velvet-black. Side, top and back of head metallic green. Occipital and nuchal feathers curled up. Middle back, rump, and upper tail-coverts silver-white. Fifth quill longest. (H. & M. i. 135.)

Note.—The Moonals, Pucras, and Snow-Cocks are made a separate subfamily by Gray.

Genus **CERIORNIS.**

κηρός = wax; ὄρνις = a bird.

Crested head partly naked, with two horns and gular wattle. Black tail of 18 feathers.—*Male* plumage red, with white spots. The Argus Pheasants of sportsmen.

805. Ceriornis satyra. THE INDIAN CRIMSON TRAGOPAN OR HORNED PHEASANT.

σάτυρος = a satyr, companion of Bacchus; at first represented with long pointed ears, a goat's tail, and small knobs, like horns, behind the ears.

Loongee, *Kumaon*; **Moonal,** *Nepal*; **Nunal,** *Sikkim*; **Dafia,** *Bengal.*

♂ 26″ to 28½″; 4½ lbs. ♀ 21½″ to 24″; 2¼ to 2½ lbs. Legs yellow-brown. Bill brown. Orbits blue. Gular wattle orange. Horns blue. Crest black in front, red behind. Above brown, finely barred black, with white spots. On wing-coverts white spotted on red. Neck, breast, and below crimson, with white spots edged black.—*Female* brown, with dark mottlings. White lines below, increasing in size from breast to vent.

806. Ceriornis melanocephalus. THE WESTERN TRAGOPAN OR HORNED PHEASANT.

μέλας = black; κεφαλή = a head.

Jewar, *Garhwal*; **Jaghi,** *Bussahir*; **Sing-moonal,** *N.W. Himalaya*; **Fulgoor,** *Chamba.*

♂ 27″ to 29″; 4½ lbs. ♀ 24″; 2¼ to 2½ lbs. Legs ashy. Bill black. Orbits bright red. Gular wattle purple. Horns sky-blue. Crest tipped red. Above brown, irregularly barred and spotted white on black. Breast and below black, dashed dull red, with white spot.—*Female* above mottled with streaks of pale yellow. Below ashy brown, powdered black, and irregular white spots.—*Young*: Second year head and neck red.

Ceriornis blythi. THE GREY-BELLIED TRAGOPAN OR HORNED PHEASANT.

♂ 21″ to 23″. ♀ 18″ to 20″. Legs light brown. Orbital skin orange. Horns azure. Forehead black. Nape and breast maroon. Abdomen creamy, with brown markings. Above brown, spotted white. —*Female* black, freckled buff. (H. & M. i. 151.)

Genus **ITHAGENES.**

ἰθαγενής = well-known.

Lower plumage grass-green, with blood-red stains. Tail of 14 feathers. Several spurs.

807. Ithagenes cruentus. THE BLOOD-PHEASANT.

Cruentŭs, a, um = bloody, gory, blood-stained.
Selmung, *Nepal*; **Soomong-pho,** *Sikkim*.

♂ 17″ to 19½″; 1 to 1¼ lb. ♀ 16½″ to 17″; 12 oz. to 1 lb. Legs coral-red. Bill black. Crest grey. Orbital skin scarlet. Above dark grey, with buff on black stripe down each feather. Throat red. Breast and below pale green, blotched blood-red.—*Female* brown, finely mottled. Forehead black. Cheeks and chin rusty yellow.

Genus PUCRASIA.

Double and central drooping crest. Moderate spur. Tail of 16 feathers. Plumage lanceolate and cock-like.

808. Pucrasia macrolopha. THE KOKLASS PHEASANT.

μακρός = long; *λόφος* = crest.
Phokrass, *Kumaon*; **Koklass,** *Simla*; **Koak,** *Kulu*; **Plas,** *Kashmir*.

♂ 23″ to 25″; 2⅛ to 3 lbs. ♀ 20″ to 22″; 2 lbs. Legs ashy. Bill black.—*Male*: Head dark green. Crown ashy. Large white spot on side of neck. Above light ashy, with long black streaks. Breast and below chestnut.—*Female*: Above pale brown, varied and barred with brown. Below light chestnut, with dark markings.

Pucrasia nipalensis. THE NEPAL KOKLASS PHEASANT.

Pokrass, *Nepal*.

♂ 24″; 2 lbs. ♀ 21″; 1½ to 2 lbs. Legs bluish grey. Bill dusky. Mantle, sides of neck, and flank-feathers striated black, chestnut, and grey.

Pucrasia castanea is added (S. F. v. 188).

Genus PHASIANUS.

Phāsiānus = *φασιανός*, the Phasian bird in Aristophanes; from the river Phasis, in Colchis, whence it is said to have been first brought by the Argonautic expedition.

True Pheasants. Tail elongated, of 18 feathers. Cheeks naked, red. —*Male* with spur.

809. **Phasianus wallichi.** The Cheer Pheasant.

Kahir, Chihir, *Nepal*; **Cheer,** *Kumaon*; **Bunchil,** *Mussoorie*; **Chaman,** *Chamba.*

♂ 34″ to 40″, tail from vent 20″ to 23″; 3 to 3½ lbs. ♀ 24″ to 30″, tail from vent 13½″ to 15½″; 2 to 3 lbs. Legs brown. Bill pale horny. Head dark ashy. Throat, breast, shoulders, and wing-coverts yellowish, with curving black bars. Median tail long, barred and blotched; below dusky.—*Female*: Head, neck, and throat with dusky oval spots. Back minutely mottled. Chin plain.

Other True Pheasants besides the English one, *P. colchicus*, are *P. torquatus*, ring-necked, of China; *P. mongolicus*; *P. versicolor*, from Japan, has interbred with Common and Ringed Pheasants in England; *P. reevesi* from China; *P. sœmmerringi* from Japan.

The Golden Pheasants form a distinct group, with crested head, neck, ruff or tippet, and very long tail. *Thaumalea picta*, from China, extends as far west as Orenburg, and was deemed by Cuvier to be the type of *Phœnix* of the ancients; *T. amherstiæ*, from Manchuria.

Genus **EUPLOCAMUS.**

εὐπλόκαμος = well curled, having many locks.

Head more or less crested. Plumage glossy black and white. Neck and breast hackled. Tail of 16 feathers, curving outwards.

810. **Euplocamus albocristatus.** The White-crested Kalij Pheasant.

Kalij, *Kumaon*; **Kookera,** *Mussoorie*; **Kaleysur,** *Kullu*; **Kolsa,** *Punjab.*

♂ 24″ to 29″; 2½ lbs. ♀ 20″ to 23″; 1¼ to 2¼ lbs. Legs grey-brown. Bill greenish.—*Male*: Head, neck, wings, and tail blue-black. Rump dull white, slightly barred. Eye-patch crimson. Throat and breast hackled light grey; below dark grey.—*Female* light brown, with feathers tipped darker. Chin whitish.—*Young* assume full plumage in first year.

Euplocamus leucomelanus. The Nepal Kalij Pheasant.

Kalich, Rechabo, *Nepal.*

♂ 23″ to 26″, tail from vent 10¾″ to 12″; 1¾ to 2½ lbs. ♀ 19″ to 20½″; 1¼ to 2 lbs. Legs brown. Bill greenish. Orbital skin crimson. Small black crest. Rump and upper tail-coverts dark green, white-tipped. Feathers of throat and breast grey-white and lanceolate. (H. & M. i. 191.)

811. Euplocamus melanonotus. THE BLACK-BACKED KALIJ PHEASANT.

♂ 21″ to 25″, tail from vent 9½″ to 12⅓″; 2¼ to 3 lbs. ♀ 15″ to 21″, tail from vent 8″ to 8¾″; 2 to 2¼ lbs. Legs horny brown. Bill pale yellow.—*Male*: Above glossy black. Breast hackled white. Abdomen dull black. No white on rump. Orbital skin bright red.—*Female* brown, with feathers white-shafted, tipped grey on back, and broadly edged white below.

Euplocamus horsfieldi. THE BLACK-BREASTED KALIJ PHEASANT.

Doreek, *Debrugurh*; **Durug**, *Garo Hills*; **Muthoora**, *Sylhet*; **Mathura**, *Chittagong*.

♂ 23″ to 24½″; 2½ to 3 lbs. ♀ 21″ to 22½″; 2 to 2½ lbs. Legs plumbeous. Bill greenish. Back and rump white. Entire lower surface and neck-feathers black, with blue-black patches. Lower back, rump, and upper tail fringed white. Coverts and long scapulars white-tipped. Orbital skin crimson. (H. & M. i. 197.)

Euplocamus cuvieri. THE ARACAN SILVER KALIJ PHEASANT.

Rak, *Aracan*; **Yit** (Burmese).

In males no white central stripes to any feathers. Tips of neck-feathers patched glossy blue-black; rest of feathers freckled.—*Female*: Back and wings olive-brown, closely freckled. Tail rufous. (H. & M. i. 201.)

Euplocamus crawfurdi. CRAWFURD'S SILVER KALIJ PHEASANT.

♂ 30″; 2¾ lbs. Legs pink. Bill pale blue. Markings of upper surface bold, and parallel to margins of feathers. Whole of central tail-feathers, except the tips and margins of inner webs, variegated black and white. (H. & M. i. 203.)

Euplocamus lineatus. THE VERMICELLATED KALIJ PHEASANT.

Lineo, avi, atum = to fashion to a straight line.
Kayit (Burmese); **Phoogyk**, *Burma*.

♂ 25½″ to 30″; 2½ to 3 lbs. 20″ to 24″; 2 to 2½ lbs. Legs pinkish brown. Bill greenish horny. Facial skin blood-red. Above, and nearly whole tail, black, finely zigzagged by white. Chin and throat black. Below black, with white shafts.—*Female*: Above pale olive-brown, with white across head, and with bars on side of neck. Below chestnut, with white shafts. (S. F. iii. 166.)

Euplocamus vieilloti. THE FIREBACK KALIJ PHEASANT.

Knokwah, *Siam*; **Mooah-mooah** (Malay).

♂ 27″ to 29″; 4½ to 5 lbs. ♀ 23″ to 24″; 3 to 3½ lbs. Legs vermilion. Bill white. Black plumage. Back fiery red, and median tail white. Head slightly crested. Orbits blue.

Subfamily GALLINÆ. JUNGLE- or SPUR-FOWL.

Head sometimes with fleshy crests or wattles. Tail compressed, usually of 14 feathers.

Inhabit India and its islands, including Ceylon and Malayana. Gray includes under this head Tragopans, Firebacks, and Kalij Pheasants of Jerdon.

Genus GALLUS.

Gallus = a cock.

Naked crest. Face nude, with wattles. Long curved spur. Forked tail semi-erect. Upper tail-coverts lengthened and curved. Neck-feathers hackled.

812. Gallus ferrugineus. THE RED JUNGLE-FOWL.

Ferrūgineus = of the colour of iron-dust, dusky.

Jungli-moorghi, Ban-moorghi, *Upper India*; **Bunkokra,** *Sundarbans*; **Pazoktchi,** *Sikhim*; **Gera-gogor,** *Gondwara*; **Lall,** *Chanda*; **Tanquet,** *Burmah*; **Ayamootan,** *Malay*.

♂ 25″ to 28″, tail from vent 11″ to 14″; 1¾ to 2¼ lbs. ♀ 16″ to 18″, tail from vent 5½″ to 6½″; 1⅛ to 1⅝ lbs. Gold hackles on head, neck, and breast. Ear-coverts white. Back purple. Sides and upper tail-coverts orange. Wing-coverts black, glossed green. Below black.—*Female* yellow, minutely mottled dark brown. Red throat line passing up behind ear. No comb or wattles.

813. Gallus sonnerati. THE GREY OR MADRAS JUNGLE-FOWL.

Komri, *Abu*; **Jungli-murghi,** *India*; **Pardah, Komri,** *Chandah*; **Kombadi,** *Deccan*; **Katu-Koli** (Tamil); **Koli,** *Mysore*.

♂ 28″ to 32″, tail from vent 14″ to 16″; 1⅝ to 2½ lbs. ♀ 18″ to 20″, tail from vent 6″ to 7″; 1½ to 1¾ lbs. Legs yellowish. Bill yellowish. Grey hackles, with yellow spots; each feather blackish, with shaft white and two spots, the terminal one like wax. Ear-coverts rufous. Plumage black and grey, with white shafts. Wing-coverts with oblong wood-brown spots.—*Female*: Above mottled brown. Below black-brown, broadly centred pure white.

Gallus lafayetti. THE CEYLON JUNGLE-FOWL.

Wali-kukula, *Ceylon.*

♂ 19″ to 25″, tail from vent 8″ to 14″; 2⅛ to 2¼ lbs. ♀ 15″ to 16″, tail from vent 5″ to 6″; 1⅛ to 1⅜ lbs. Face, comb, and wattles purplish red, with yellow oval spot. Above red. Below red. Tail purple.—*Female* brown mottled, each feather margined dark brown. Chin white. (H. & M. i. 243.)

Genus GALLOPERDIX. SPUR-FOWL.

Gallus = a cock ; πέρδιξ = Partridge in classical authors.

Of small size. Nude orbits. No comb or wattles. Two or more spurs. Erect tail, folded.—*Female* one or more spurs.

814. Galloperdix spadiceus. THE RED SPUR-FOWL.

Chota jungli murghi, *C. P.*; **Kustoor**, *Deccan*; **Sarava-koli** (Tamil); **Yerra kodi** (Telugu).

♂ 14″ to 15″; 11 to 14 oz. ♀ 13″ to 14½″; 9 to 12 oz. Legs vermilion. Bill dusky. Head olive-brown. Chin and throat pale brown. Body and central tail chestnut. Below olive.—*Female* : Crown dusky. Neck olive. Above brown banded black, minutely speckled. Breast red, tipped black. Below dusky.

Galloperdix lunulatus. THE PAINTED SPUR-FOWL.

Lūnŭlatus, *lūnŭla*, *æ*, f. = a little moon, an ornament worn by women.
Askol, *Orissa*; **Hootkah**, *Chanda*; **Cull-koli** (Tamil); **Jitta-kodi** (Telugu).

♂ 12″ to 13½″; 9 to 10 oz. ♀ 12″ to 12½″; 8 to 9 oz. Legs horny brown. Bill blackish. Head and neck black, with white streaks and spots. Above chestnut, with white spots. Breast buff, with black triangular marks.—*Female* dull olive-brown. Nape chestnut. Pale ruff and moustache.—*Young* have the female plumage, with tertiaries and tail chestnut banded black. Young females partly spotted black.

Galloperdix bicalcaratus. THE CEYLON SPUR-FOWL.

♂ 12½″ to 14½″; 11 to 13 oz. ♀ 11″ to 11¼″; 7 to 10 oz. Legs pale red. Bill pale red. Below mottled black and white. Back chestnut. Tail black. *Males* generally have four and sometimes six spurs. Wing-coverts chestnut, spotted white.—*Female* brown, with red eye-patch. Seldom devoid of spurs, and often have two or three. (H. & M. i. 261.)

Subfamily MELEAGRINÆ.

This includes the Turkeys from the Northern Continent of America and the Guinea-fowls from Africa. Fifth remex present in Turkey's wing.

Family TETRAONIDÆ. GROUSE and PARTRIDGES.

Wings rounded in most. Bill and tail very short. Hind toe elevated. Plumage game. Differ slightly in sexes. Frequent grass and low jungle.

Subfamily PERDICINÆ.

Tarsus nude, often spurred and scaled. Bill short, strong, and very convex. Moderate or small size.

Genus **TETRAOGALLUS.** SNOW-COCKS.

τετράων = proper name; *gallus* = a cock.

Naked eye-patch. Second and third quills longest. Tail of 18 feathers. Blunt spur. Confined to Highlands of Central Asia and Himalayas.

816. Tetraogallus himalayensis. THE HIMALAYAN SNOW-COCK.

Kullu, *Nepal*; **Jer-moonal**, *Mussoorie*; **Leep**, *Kulu*; **Kubuk**, *Cashmir*; **Kank-i-durra**, *Afghanistan*; **Kabk-i-dareh**, *Persia*; **Utar**, *Turkistan*.

♂ 26″ to 29″; 5 to 6½ lbs. ♀ 21″ to 24″; 3 to 4 lbs. Legs yellow-red. Bill pale horny. Ashy grey, minutely freckled. Primaries white, tipped dusky. Undertail white. Chestnut bands from eye and mouth meet and form a collar.—*Male* has a blunt spur; *female* has none.

Tetraogallus tibetanus. THE THIBETAN SNOW-COCK.

Huinwal, Ular (Kirghiz); **Hailik** (Mongol); **Cunmo** (Tanguts).

♂ 19″ to 21½″. ♀ 18″. Legs ♂ coral, ♀ orange. Bill ♂ orange-red, ♀ blackish, orange tip. Pale grey tinged pink, fine freckled. Primaries French grey, tipped white. Undertail black. White wing-band. Gorget freckled grey and buff.—*Female*: Ear-coverts white. ('Lahore to Yarkand,' p. 281.)

Genus **LERWA.** Snow-Partridge.

Lerwar = vox barbara.

Orbits plumed. Wing expansive and second quill longest. Tarsi slightly feathered. Tail of 14 feathers.

817. Lerwa nivicola. The Snow-Partridge.

Larwa, *Nepal*; **Jungooria,** *Kumaon*; **Koor-monal,** *Garhwal*; **Barf-ka-titur,** *Kulu.*

♂ 14″ to 16″; 16 to 22 oz. Legs red. Bill bright red. Minutely barred black and grey.—*Male* has short spurs.—*Female* like the male, but no spurs.

Genus **FRANCOLINUS.**

Francolinus = proper name.

Rich spotted plumage. Tail of 14 feathers, even or rounded.—*Male* with strong blunt spur.

818. Francolinus vulgaris. The Common Francolin or Black Meadow-Partridge.

Kala-titur, *Nepal*; **Tetra,** *Garhwal*; **Vrembi,** *Manipur*; **Taroo,** *Afghanistan.*

Khairadera, 12-10-72.

♂ $12\frac{3}{4}''$ to $14\frac{1}{2}''$; 10 to 20 oz. ♀ $12\frac{1}{4}''$ to 14″; 8 to 17 oz. Legs yellow. Bill black. Head black. White ear-patch. Chestnut collar. —*Female*: Plumage below white, with black spots arrow-shaped.

819. Francolinus pictus. THE PAINTED FRANCOLIN OR SOUTHERN MEADOW-PARTRIDGE.

Titur, *Deccan*; **Kakora-kodi** (Telugu).

♂ 11″ to 13″; 8½ to 13 oz. Legs yellow-red. Bill blackish. Head and neck chestnut. No spurs.—*Female*: Lower plumage variegated black and white.

Francolinus chinensis. THE CHINESE FRANCOLIN OR EASTERN MEADOW-PARTRIDGE.

Hka, *Pegu*; **Nock-kahtah,** *Siam*.

♂ 12″ to 13½″; 10 to 14 oz. Legs brown-orange. Bill black. Crown dark brown. Black eye-streak. Neck, wing-coverts, sides, and breast black, with a row of oval white or buffy spots on each web of every feather. Comparatively large spur.—*Female*: Feathers regularly and closely barred black and fulvous white. (H. & M. ii. 27.)

Genus **CACCABIS.**

Caccăbis = κακκαβίς, a collateral form of κακκάβη, a Partridge, in classical Greek.

Nude eye-patch. Plumage not mottled.

820. Caccabis chukor. THE CHUKOR OR REDLEG, OR ROCK-PARTRIDGE.

Khojak, 2–6–79.

Kaukau, *Kashmir*; **Keklik,** *Yarkand*; **Kabk,** *Persia*.

♂ $14\frac{1}{4}''$ to $16''$; 19 to 27 oz. ♀ $13''$ to $14\frac{1}{2}''$; 13 to 19 oz. Legs red. Bill red. Black necklace from eye round throat. Breast and belly banded.—*Female* same as male, but no spurs.

Genus **AMMOPERDIX.**

Of small size. No spur.

821. Ammoperdix bonhami. The Seesee or Sand-Partridge.

Sisi, *Punjab*; **Tihu,** *Persia.*

♂ $9\frac{1}{2}''$ to $11''$; 7 to 8 oz. ♀ $9''$ to $9\frac{3}{4}''$; 6 to 8 oz. Legs olive-yellow. Bill pink. Pale brown freckled. Breast grey. Black streak from

Chaman, 31-5-79.

forehead across eye to behind the ear. Neck blue-grey spotted white. —*Female* grey, finely mottled all over. (H. & M. ii. 45.)

Genus **ORTYGORNIS.**

Ortyx = ὄρτυξ = the Quail, in classical Greek; from the root of *verto* = I turn, from its whirling flight. Cf. Sanskrit *vartakas* = a Quail, *vart* = to roll. ὄρνις = a bird.

Tip of bill well turned over. Tail of 12 feathers.

822. Ortygornis pondicerianus. The Grey or Spurred, or Bush-Partridge.

Titur, *India*; **Goujul-haki,** *Mysore*; **Kondari** (Tamil); **Kuwunzu** (Telugu); **Jirufti** (Persian).

♂ $11\frac{1}{2}''$ to $13\frac{1}{3}''$; 9 to 12 oz. ♀ $10''$ to $12''$; 7 to 11 oz. Legs bright red. Bill plumbeous. Feathers red-brown, with three bars cream-yellow.—*Female* smaller, with no spurs.

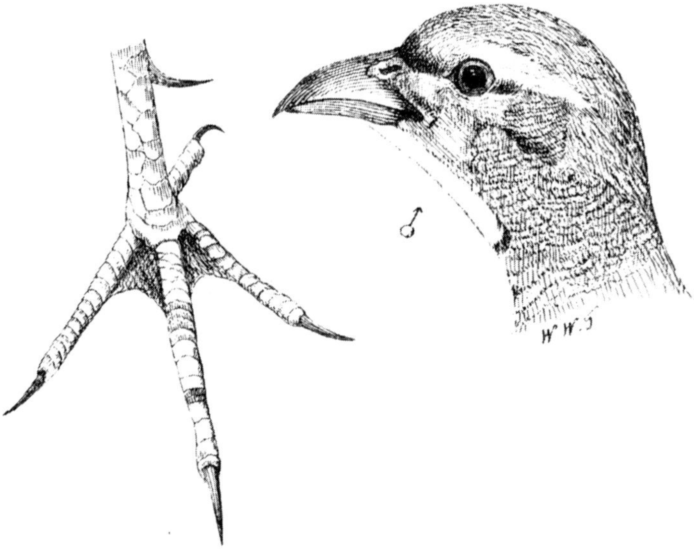

Ortygornis pondicerianus.

823. Ortygornis gularis. THE KYAH OR SWAMP-PARTRIDGE.

Kyah, *Bengal*; **Buntitur,** *India*; **Koi,** *Assam*; **Bhil-titar,** *Cachar*.

♂ 15″; 17 to 22 oz. ♀ 14″. Lower plumage brown, white streaks edged black, blotched on abdomen. Chin and throat chestnut.—*Female* smaller, with no spur.

Genus **PERDIX.**

Perdix = πέρδιξ, a Partridge, in classical authors.

No spur. Tail of 18 feathers.

Perdix hodgsoniæ. THE THIBETAN PARTRIDGE.

Sakpha, *Thibet.*

♂ 13″; 1 lb. Legs green. Bill green. Nude crimson eye-patch. Above olive-brown. Head red, with white speck. Black line from forehead. Belt of black-edged feathers below represents the horseshoe of English birds. (H. & M. ii. 66.)

This Thibet Partridge is the only representative of the true Partridge in India. The English bird (*P. cinerea*) extends, except in extreme north, pretty well all over Europe, though rarer in the south, and through Asia Minor to Western Persia. The Asiatic representative of this species, *P. barbata* (differing chiefly in its smaller size, longer and more pointed throat-feathers, and black instead of chestnut horseshoe on lower breast), which is common in S.E. Siberia, Mongolia, and N. China, extends, in our direction at any rate, to the Kokonoor Mountains and other localities in N.E. districts of Chinese Thibet.

Genus **ARBORICOLA.**

The Wood-Partridges occur throughout the Himalayas, but are found nowhere else in India proper. They extend into Assam and Burmah. One species is stated to occur in China.

Tarsus not spurred. Toes with very long claws. Tail of 12 soft feathers. Sexes alike in all except *torqueolus*.

(i.) *With upper back barred or fringed with black.*

824. Arboricola torqueolus. THE COMMON WOOD-PARTRIDGE.

Torquis or *torques* = a twisted neck-chain, necklace.
Peura, *Kumaon*; **Kaindal,** *Kangra*; **Kaugkom,** *Sikhim*.

♂ 10½″ to 12″; 13½ oz. ♀ 8 oz. Legs slate-grey. Bill black.—*Male*: Crown bright red. Breast pale ashy, below a white band.—*Female*: Breast grey, tinged rusty, with middle of throat rufous unspotted.

Arboricola atrogularis. THE BLACK-THROATED WOOD-PARTRIDGE.

Peura, *Sylhet*; **Duboy,** *Assam*; **Sanbatai,** *Chittagong*.

♂ 10″ to 11″; 7 to 10 oz. ♀ 7 to 10 oz. Legs orange-red. Bill black. Brown grey-olive, more or less black-spotted. Breast pale grey. (H. & M. ii. 79.)

Arboricola brunneopectus. THE BROWN-BREASTED WOOD-PARTRIDGE.

Tounkha, *Pegu*.

♂ 10½″ to 11½″; 9 to 13 oz. ♀ 10″ to 10⅔″; 8 to 12 oz. Legs red. Bill black. Middle of throat fawn, densely spotted black. Breast tawny. Wings strongly marked chestnut. (H. & M. ii. 87.)

Arboricola chloropus. THE GREEN-LEGGED WOOD-PARTRIDGE.

χλωρός = pale green; πούς = a foot.
Tounkha, *Pegu*.

♂ 11½″ to 12″; 9 to 12 oz. ♀ 10½″ to 11½″; 8 to 10 oz. Legs

pale green. Bill greenish. Chin, throat, and sides of neck white, spotted black, not enclosed by black band. Breast olive, banded black. (H. & M. ii. 91.)

(ii.) *With upper back not barred or fringed.*

825. Arboricola rufogularis. The Rufous-throated Wood-Partridge.

Lakom, *Sikhim*; **Pokhu,** *Daphla Hills*; **Peura,** *Kumaun.*

♂ 10″ to 11″; 7 to 10 oz. ♀ 9″ to 10½″; 7 to 10 oz. Legs red. Bill black. Lower margin of rufous throat with sharply defined black line. Breast grey. (H. & M. ii. 75.)

Arboricola mandellii. The Bhutan Wood-Partridge.

♂ 8½″. Legs red. Bill black. Lower margin of rufous throat with sharply defined black line. Breast maroon. Patch in neck pure white. (H. & M. ii. 83.)

Arboricola intermedius. The Aracan Wood-Partridge.

♂ 10″ to 11″. Legs red. Bill black. Lower margin of rufous throat meeting grey of breast, without black line. Centre of throat more or less black. (H. & M. ii. 85.)

Arboricola tickelli. The Tenasserim Wood-Partridge.

Same as *intermedius*, but centre of throat rufous, spotted black.

(iii.) *With upper back freckled and mottled.*

Arboricola charltoni. The Malayan Wood-Partridge.

♂ 10″ to 11″. Legs red. Bill black. Chin, throat, and sides of neck white, with black spots enclosed in irregular black band. (H. & M. ii. 93.)

Genus BAMBUSICOLA.

Bambusicola fytchii. The Indo-Chinese or Western Bamboo-Partridge.

Vengte (Kuki).

♂ 14″; 10 to 14 oz. ♀ 12½″ to 13½″; 9 to 12 oz. Legs plumbeous.

Bill brown. Male with spurs. Black eye-streak. Side and flank-feathers have velvet-black heart-shaped spots. Lower back and rump olive-brown, irregularly barred. Chin dark brown. Tail rufous, conspicuously banded. (H. & M. ii. 97.)

Genus **CALOPERDIX.**

Caloperdix oculeus. THE TENASSERIM OR FERRUGINOUS WOOD-PARTRIDGE.

καλός = beautiful; πέρδιξ = Partridge; *ŏcŭlus* = an eye.
Burong, Trung (Malay), *Sumatra.*

♂ 10¾″; 8 oz. Legs dirty green. Bill black. Head and breast and below chestnut. Back black, with feathers fringed white. Often double-spurred.

This genus may come in here. Might be classed with the Pea-Pheasants or Spur-fowl. It extends up the Malayan Peninsula.

Genus **ROLLULUS.**

Rollulus coronatus. THE MALAYAN CROWNED PARTRIDGE.

Remarkable for wanting the claw of the hind toe. From their colour, fan-like crest, and different colour of the sexes they might rather be placed with the Jungle-fowl than with the Partridges. The crest is similar to that of the Crowned Pigeons, and the bare frontal plumes are only represented elsewhere in this family by some of the American Partridges. (Jerdon, iii. p. 580.) Placed by Gray in *Tetraoninæ.*

♂ 10¾″ to 11″; 8 to 10 oz. ♀ 9½″ to 10½″; 8 oz. Legs red. Bill black. No spurs. Red crest. Facial skin and eyelids bright red. Head black. Below black. Back green. Wings umber.—*Female*: Black head, grass-green body, and umber wings. (H. & M. ii. 103.)

Note.—Of Bush-Quails (as shown by Jerdon) the genus *Perdicula* is peculiar to India proper, and not found to east of Bay of Bengal nor across the Indus. *Ophrysia* is obtained near about Mussoorie, and *Microperdix* on the Western Ghats and Nilghiris. As no other species is known, they are here styled JUNGLE-QUAILS (instead of Jerdon's term Bush-Quails), to avoid mixing them up with *Turnicinæ* (defined by Jerdon as Bustard and Button-Quail), which Gray calls Bush-Quails.

Genus **OPHRYSIA.**

ὀφρύς (a plant with two leaves) = an eyebrow.

♂ 10″. ♀ 10″. Legs red. Bill dull red.—*Male*: Black, head blotched white. Breast dark grey, lined black. Back tinged rufous.—*Female* brown, broadly marked black. No other species of this genus is known.

N.W. Himalayas.

Genus **PERDICULA.**

Blunt spurs. Tail of 12 feathers. Sexes differ.

826. Perdicula asiatica. The Jungle-Quail.

Lowa (Hindi); **Juhar**, *Manbhoom*; **Girza-pitta** (Telugu); **Kari lowga**, *Mysore*.

♂ $6\frac{1}{3}''$ to 7″; 2 to 3 oz. Legs yellow. Bill dusky red. Chin and eye-stripe chestnut. White superciliary stripe. Upper plumage dark red-brown. Under surface white.—*Female*: Lower plumage spotless rufous, with white shafts.

827. Perdicula argoondah. The Red or Rock Jungle-Quail.

Lowa (Hindi); **Lawunka** (Telugu); **Kemp lowga**, *Mysore*.

♂ $6\frac{2}{3}''$ to 7″; $2\frac{1}{4}$ to 3 oz. ♀ $6\frac{3}{4}''$. Legs dull red. Bill dark slaty. Head and neck rufous, tipped black. Lower plumage with black cross-bars.—*Female* rufous. Whitish on vent.

Genus **MICROPERDIX.**

μικρός = small.

Slender red bill. Male wants tarsal tubercle.

828. Microperdix erythrorhynchus. The Painted Jungle-Quail.

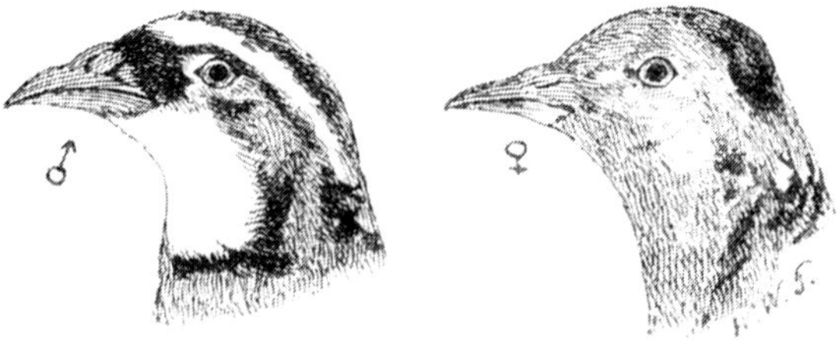

Sapoora, 9-8-75.

Kokni-lowa (Hindi): **Kadai** (Tamil).

♂ $6\frac{1}{2}''$ to $7\frac{1}{2}''$; $2\frac{1}{2}$ to 3 oz. Legs fine red. Bill fine red. Crown black. Back olive, spotted black. Chin white, with black border.—*Female*: Head brown. Chin rufous. Above olive, blotched black.

Microperdix blewitti. The Eastern Painted Jungle-Quail.

Sirsee-lowa, *Mandla, Chanda.*

♂ $6''$ to $6\frac{1}{2}''$; $1\frac{4}{5}$ to $2\frac{1}{3}$ oz. Legs coral-red. Bill coral-red. Narrow black frontal band. Breast and below chestnut, widely spotted black. Above grey.—*Female* grey, with broad pale frontal band. Sides spotted. (H. & M. ii. 129.)

Subfamily Coturnicinæ. True Quails.

Genus COTURNIX.

Coturnix = a Quail, in classical Latin. Etymology unknown.

Wings pointed. No spur.

True Quail are most common in S. Asia, but occur throughout the whole of the Old Continent as far as New Zealand. The Grey Quail is found throughout the greater part of Asia, Europe, and Africa. The Rain-Quail extends to Assam, Sylhet, and Upper Burma. Of the Blue Quail, one species occurs in India and several in China, Malaya, Australia, and New Guinea; but none in Central or Western Asia or Africa. The species from Celebes (*Excalfactoria minuta*) is the smallest game bird in the World.

829. Coturnix communis. The Large Grey or European Quail.

Bateyr, *Upper India*; **Butteyra,** *Sind*; **Buttree,** *Lower Bengal*; **Soipol,** *Manipur*; **Botah-surrai,** *Assam*; **Burganji,** *Deccan*; **Burli,** *Belgaom*; **Sipalé-haki,** *Mysore*; **Watwalak,** *Kashgar.*

♂ $8\frac{1}{2}''$; 3 to $4\frac{1}{2}$ oz. ♀ 4 oz. Legs fleshy pink. Bill grey-brown. Double collar. Lower plumage pale rufous. Primaries barred.—*Female* larger than male, with brown spots on breast.—*Young* birds ashy.

Sykes, Yarrell, and others say this was the Quail of the Israelites. (See no. 801.)

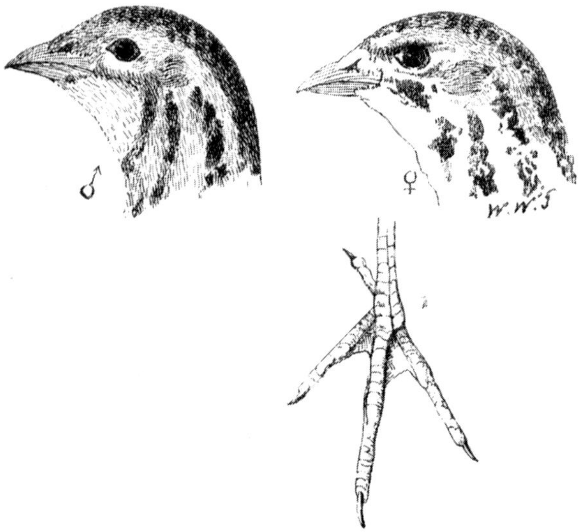

Coturnix communis.

830. Coturnix coromandelicus. THE BLACK-BREASTED OR RAIN-QUAIL.

Bateyr, *Upper India*; **Chanac,** *Nepal*; **Butteyra,** *Sind*; **Ngon,** *Pegu.*

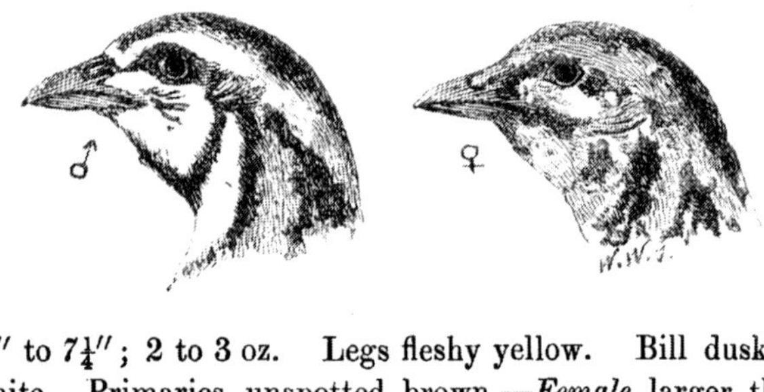

♂ $6\frac{1}{2}''$ to $7\frac{1}{4}''$; 2 to 3 oz. Legs fleshy yellow. Bill dusky. Chin pure white. Primaries unspotted brown.—*Female* larger than male, wants black breast and cross-bar.

Call *whit*! *whit*! Stronger than the Grey.

Genus **EXCALFACTORIA.**

Excalfactorius, a, um = warming, heating.

Rich plumage. Second quill longest.

831. Excalfactoria chinensis. THE BLUE-BREASTED OR PAINTED QUAIL.

Khair-butai, *Nepal*; **Peeyo,** *Malay.*

♂ 5¾″ to 6″; 1½ to 2 oz. ♀ 5″. Legs bright yellow. Bill black. Red wing-band. Quills barred black. Breast dark purple.—*Female* brown; breast with dark cross-bars.

Subfamily ODONTOPHORINÆ. AMERICAN PARTRIDGES.

There are four genera :—1. *Odontophorus,* found in tropical forests of America; 2. *Cyrtonix,* peculiar to Mexico; 3. *Ortyx,* ranges through N. and S. America, Jamaica, and W.-I. Isles; 4. is found in California and Mexico, up lochs, on sandy plains or open wood.

Subfamily TETRAONINÆ. TRUE GROUSE.

Not represented in India, being peculiar to northern parts of both Continents. The best known are *T. scoticus* (the Scottish Grouse), *T. tetrix* (the Blackcock), *T. urogallus* (the noble Capercailzie), *Lagopus mutus* (the mountain-loving Ptarmigan). Several other species of Grouse occur both on the continent of Europe and N. Asia, and one species of Ptarmigan occurs in the Caucasus; but as yet no species of Grouse or Ptarmigan has been observed on the Himalayas or adjacent territories. The Ruffed Grouse of Europe (*Bonasia sylvestris*) descends to a lower latitude than any of the true Grouse. One group, called "Pintailed Pheasants," is peculiar to N. America.

Family TURNICIDÆ.

Note.—The family is here given as *Turnicidæ,* in place of Jerdon's *Tinamidæ,* because the subfamily have nothing to do with *Tinamidæ,* which are restricted by Gray to S. America.

Bill slender. Wings moderate. Tail short or none. Lateral toes short. No spurs. Hind toe small or none. Frequent bushes and grass-jungle.

Subfamily TURNICINÆ. BUSTARD and BUTTON-QUAIL.

Of diminutive size. Three toes in one genus. Hind toe in another.

Note.—Bustard-Quails differ more from Quails than the latter do from Peafowl in structure.

Genus TURNIX.

Turnix, shortened from *Coturnix*, q. v., to show that it was a mutilated form, wanting the hind toe.

First quill as long as others. No hind toe. Tail very short, of 12 feathers in a bundle.

(i.) *Female black, barred on throat and breast.*

832. Turnix taigoor. THE INDIAN BUSTARD-QUAIL.

Gulu, *India*; **Durwa,** *Rutnagiri*; **Karehaki,** *Mysore.*

Sapoora, 9–8–75.

♂ $5\frac{1}{2}''$ to $6\frac{1}{3}''$; $1\frac{1}{2}$ to 2 oz. ♀ $6''$ to $6\frac{1}{2}''$; $1\frac{1}{2}$ to $2\frac{1}{4}$ oz. Legs plumbeous. Bill dark slaty. Chin and throat black. Breast faintly banded. —*Female*: Transverse black lines on back.

833. Turnix plumbipes. THE HILL OR INDO-MALAYAN BUSTARD-QUAIL.

Timokpho (Lepcha); **Ngon,** *Pegu*; **Gnoke-coone,** *Malaya.*

♂ $5\frac{1}{2}''$ to $6\frac{1}{4}''$; $1\frac{1}{2}$ to 2 oz. ♀ $6''$ to $7''$; $\frac{1}{2}$ to 2 oz. Legs leaden. Bill slaty. Chin black. Black wing-spots, rounded.—*Female*: Back minutely mottled.

(ii.) *Sexes nearly alike. Plumage more or less spotted.*

Turnix maculosa. THE BURMO-MALAYAN BUTTON-QUAIL.

Ngon, *Pegu.*

♂ $6\frac{1}{2}''$ to $7''$; $2\frac{1}{4}$ oz. ♀ $2\frac{3}{4}$ oz. Legs chrome-yellow. Bill red-brown. Chin, throat, and abdomen white. Breast rufous-buff. Side-feathers with round black spots. (H. & M. ii. 183.)

834. Turnix joudera. THE LARGER BUTTON-QUAIL.

Lowa, *Upper India*; **Pedda-dubba-gúndlú** (Telugu).

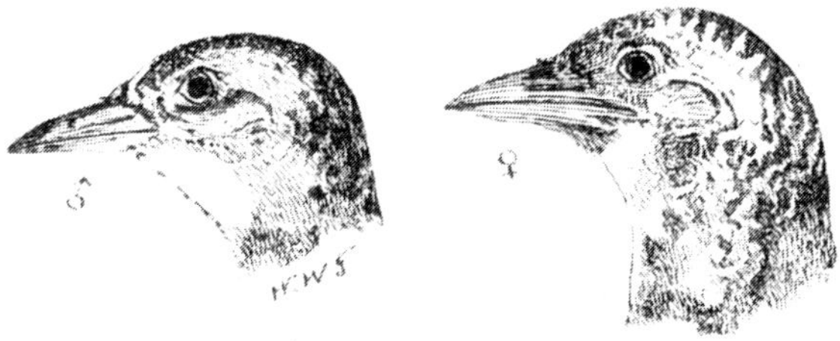

♂ 6″; $1\frac{1}{8}$ to $1\frac{1}{2}$ oz. Legs deep yellow. Bill yellow. Wing-coverts light brown, with small black spot margined yellow. Seen singly.

Jerdon wrongly names this *dussumieri*.

835. Turnix dussumieri. THE BUTTON-QUAIL.

Chota Lowa, *India*; **Chimraj,** *Muttra*; **Tatu-bateyra,** *Sind*; **Durwi,** *Ratnagiri*; **Sán-gúndlú,** *Orissa*.

Sapoora, 9-8-75.

♂ 5″ to $5\frac{1}{2}$″; 1 to $1\frac{1}{3}$ oz. ♀ $5\frac{1}{2}$″ to $5\frac{2}{3}$″; $1\frac{1}{4}$ to $1\frac{1}{2}$ oz. Legs fleshy white. Bill plumbeous. Head brown, barred black. Chin and throat pure white. Abdomen whitish. Rise once only. Single note.

Turnix albiventris. THE NICOBAR BUTTON-QUAIL.

Mool, *Gamorta*.

♂ 6″; $1\frac{1}{4}$ oz. ♀ $6\frac{1}{2}$″; $1\frac{3}{4}$ oz. Legs yellow. Bill yellow. Broad half-collar chestnut. Two black stripes from crown to nape. Outer web of first primary nearly white. (H. & M. ii. 199.)

Family CHIONIDIDÆ.

Subfamily CHIONIDINÆ. SHEATHBILLS.

One genus, *Chionis*; singular birds in the islands of the Antarctic and at southern extremity of South America. *C. alba* (the Kelp-Pigeon) lives on coasts of Australia and New Zealand.

Family TINAMIDÆ.

Subfamily TINAMINÆ. TINAMOUS.

Given by Gray as the first and only subfamily. There are four genera:—*Tinamus, Nothura, Rhynchotus*, and *Tinamotis*.

GRALLATORES.

SHORE BIRDS.

Order.	Sub-order.	Tribe.	F
GRALLATORES. (WALKERS OR WADERS.) *SHORE BIRDS.* Lower part of tibia bare. Tarsus elongated. Wings usually long. Tail usually short. Bill straight or inclining. Outer toe usually joined to middle one by short web, and to inner toe occasionally. In a few, toes are bordered by loose web. ALL FLY WELL, WITH LEGS OUT BEHIND.	Young, when hatched, able to run at once.	*STRUTHIONES.*—Of large size. Some with three toes, others with only two. Wings undeveloped	**STRUTHIONIDÆ.**—Bil short or imperfect. To varying from two to fou
		PRESSIROSTRES.—Bill thick and compressed. Tarsi long. Hind toe small or absent	**OTIDIDÆ.**—Bill short, with connecting membı game-like ....
			CURSORIDÆ.—Bill so only. Plumage brown
			GLAREOLIDÆ.—Bill s Gape very large. Tail
			CHARADRIIDÆ.—Bill nasal groove. Wings lo Hind toe generally want
			HÆMATOPODIDÆ.— the others. Plumage birds ....
			THINOCORIDÆ.—Pur
			GRUIDÆ.—Bill short, cleft. Large size. Pl neck ....
		LONGIROSTRES.—Bill long and slender. Hallux short or raised. Exterior toe generally joined to middle by web	**SCOLOPACIDÆ.**—Bill long. Tail short. Plu ashy beneath. Hind to
			HIMANTOPIDÆ.—Bill times recurved. Plum long ....
		LATITORES.—Feet very large. Hind toe large. Wings short, often spurred	**PALAMEDEIDÆ.**—Am
			PARRIDÆ.—Feet enorn spurred ....
			RALLIDÆ.—Bill short feet. Tail short or none spur ....
	Young helpless at birth.	*CULTIROSTRES.*—Bill thick, pointed or slightly curved. Wings ample. Hind toe on same plane as anterior	**CICONIIDÆ.**—Bill larg toes joined at base. Of
			ARDEIDÆ.—Bill very s toe only joined to midd less serrated ....
			TANTALIDÆ.—Bill h curved. Front toes joi

* Not repr

ly.	Subfamily.	Genus.	Page.
f various forms. Wings short, broad, unequal, and number	STRUTHIONINÆ	OSTRICHES* .... RHEAS* .... EMUS* .... CASSOWARIES*	39 39 39 39
	APTERYGINÆ	APTERYX*	40
ight. Three short toes, . Plumage mottled and ;	....	BUSTARDS.................... FLORIKINS	41 42
what slender. Three toes rufous	....	COURIER-PLOVERS	44
, arched. Small hind toe. iforked................	....	SWALLOW-PLOVERS or PRATINCOLES......................	45
rt, basal half soft. Long and pointed. Gape small.	CHARADRIINÆ ...... VANELLINÆ.......... ESACINÆ	TRUE PLOVERS .... LAPWINGS .... STONE-CURLEWS..............	47 50 52
ll hind toe raised above egated. Chiefly sea-shore	STREPSILINÆ .... DROMADINÆ.......... HÆMATOPODINÆ	TURNSTONES .... CRAB-PLOVERS .... OYSTER-CATCHERS	54 55 55
American	THINOCORINÆ........	GAME PLOVERS or SHORE-LARKS*	58
ut, straight, and slightly ge grey or white. Long	....	CRANES......................	58
g, slender, soft. Wings e brown above, white or enerally elevated	SCOLOPACINÆ........	WOODCOCKS .... TRUE SNIPES	60 60
	LIMOSINÆ	GODWITS	64
	NUMENINÆ	CURLEWS....................	68
	TRINGINÆ............	STINTS	70
	PHALAROPINÆ	PHALAROPES or LOBEFOOTS	73
	TOTANINÆ............	SANDPIPERS.................. GREENSHANKS .... REDSHANKS..................	74 75 75
ry long, very thin, some- black and white. Legs	....	STILTS .... AVOCETS	77 77
can....................	PALAMEDEINÆ	SCREAMERS*	78
s. Claws strong. Wings	PARRINÆ	JACANAS	78
d wedge-shaped. Large Wing rounded, often with	GALLINULINÆ........	COOTS .... WATER-COCKS................ WATER-HENS	80 81 81
	RALLINÆ	TRUE RAILS..................	83
ong, straight. All anterior ge size	....	STORKS......................	86
p and deeply cleft. Outer one. Middle toe more or	PSOPHINÆ............	TRUMPETERS*................	87
	ARDEINÆ	HERONS .... EGRETS...................... BITTERNS.................... NIGHT-HERONS	88 89 92 93
, long, cylindrical, and at base by web	TANTALINÆ.......... PLATALEINÆ .... ANASTOMATINÆ...... IBISINÆ	PELICAN IBISES .... SPOONBILL IBISES .... SHELL IBISES .... TRUE IBISES	93 94 94 94

ited in India.

Order GRALLATORES. *SHORE BIRDS.*

Waders.

The term Grallatores (derived from *grădĭor*, to take steps) is applied by ornithologists to the Shore Birds, from their stalking, walking, or wading. Shore Birds frequent edges of rivers, seas, lakes, and a few dry plains and deserts; they feed on fish, reptiles, mollusks, insects, and a few on vegetable matter. In large numbers there is a vernal moult, and plumage changes considerably, in many becoming more or less black, in others rufous.

Lower part of tibia bare. Tarsus elongated. Wings usually long. Tail usually short. Bill straight or inclining. Outer toe usually joined to middle one by short web, and to inner toe occasionally. In a few, toes are bordered by loose web. All fly well, with legs out behind.

(A) *The young, when hatched, able to run at once.*

Tribe *STRUTHIONES.*

Of large size. Some with three toes, others with only two. Wings undeveloped.

This tribe, not represented in India, includes the giants of the Bird Kingdom, and approaches nearest to *Mammalia.*

In the subfamily *Struthioninæ* there are:—The Ostrich, *S. camelus,* of the open plains of Africa (Jerdon supposes a second species, *S. epoasticus*), with two unequal toes, a middle and an outer.

The Rheas, or S.-American Ostriches, with three anterior toes (lateral toes shorter than middle, inner the shortest). Three species.

The Emus, of New Holland, with three toes, the inner the shortest. Plumage resembles hair. Wings more rudimentary than in Ostrich. Accessory plume as large as the feather. Two species.

The Cassowaries, of the Eastern Archipelago, with three toes, the outer the longest, and the inner armed with a powerful claw. Plumage hair-like. Accessory plume very large, and a rudiment of a third. Four species.

It has been remarked that Emus and Cassowaries resemble Bustards in their anatomy, while the Ostrich and Rheas are more like Game Birds. Owen says Cassowaries are modified Coots, and Parker states there is a connection between Rails and the Ostrich.

In the subfamily *Apteryginæ* there is the *Apteryx* of New Zealand. Wingless, and feathers want the supplementary plume. Three species.

Fragments of some enormous birds have been discovered in New Zealand. One, a Moa, lately supposed extinct, its egg larger than that of an Ostrich. Fossil remains of a gigantic Ostrich have been found in the Sewalik range.

Tribe *PRESSIROSTRES.* Bustards, Plovers, and Cranes.

Pressus, a, um, adj. = compressed; *rostrum, i,* n. = the bill.

Bill thick and compressed. Tarsi long. Hind toe small or absent.

Family OTIDIDÆ. Bustards and Florikins.

Bill short, straight. Three short toes, with connecting membrane. Plumage mottled and game-like.

Bustards and Florikins are found on grassy plains of the Old World and Australia. They have the aspect and form of Game Birds, but their general anatomy allies them with Plovers. In some there is a gular membranous pouch. They can raise ear-feathers to catch sound.

The European Bustard is found throughout Central Europe and Central Asia; once shot at Hashtnagar (H. & M. i. 1). The Little Bustard occurs in Punjab and N. W. P.; is common in S. Europe and N. Africa, and occurs from Syria to Biluchistan; does not appear to go N. across Tianshan or into China.

Eupodotis occurs in India, China, Africa, and Australia (wild Turkey).

Houbara, from N. Africa, occasionally passes into Spain; one species in N. W. P., and common in Afghanistan.

Genus **OTIS.**

ὠτίς = a kind of Bustard with long ear-feathers, known to the Greeks; from *οὖς*, genit. *ὠτός*, an ear.

Short and stout limbs and bill. Long white moustachial tuft.

Otis tarda. The Great or European Bustard.

Tarda, the Spanish name, according to Pliny (Hist. Nat. x. p. 29). A Celtic or Basque word. *Tarda* and *Bistarda* are always used as substantives, like the French *Outarde* (from *avis tarda*, through the Provençal *Austarde*, as *avis struthio* became *Autruche* in French and Ostrich in English) and our *Bus-tard*.

♂ 45″; 20 to 30 lbs. ♀ 36″. Legs blackish. Bill brown.—*Male*: Chin white, with long narrow feathers. Breast pale orange. Back orange, barred black.—*Female* without chin-plume till third or fourth year.—*Young* born buff-colour, barred black.

Otis tetrax. The Little or Butterfly Bustard.

Tĕtrax = τέτραξ, a bird known to the ancient Greeks.

♂ 17″ to 19″; 1½ to 2 lbs. Legs yellow. Bill brown.—*Male*: Neck and upper breast black, with white necklet and white gorget. Breast white. Back chestnut, streaked black irregularly. Tail of 18 feathers. —*Female*: Head and neck chestnut, mottled black. Breast with short black bars.

Genus **EUPODOTIS.**

εὖ = well; ποδοτής = footed.

Long strong legs.—*Male* with pouch. Crest black. Neck white. Of very large size.

836. Eupodotis edwardsi. The Great Indian Bustard.

Toogder, *Punjab*; **Hoom,** *C. P.*; **Kara-dhouk,** *Deccan*; **Gurahna,** *Sind*; **Heri-hakki,** *Mysore*.

♂ 45″ to 50″; 17 to 22 lbs. ♀ 36″ to 38″; 8 to 10 lbs. Legs dingy yellow. Bill dusky and yellow. Sexes alike. Plumage pale brown, variegated with minute black lines. Greater coverts grey, tipped white. Primaries slaty, tip white.—*Female*: Breast-band incomplete.—*Young* resemble females.

Genus **HOUBARA.**

The Asiatic name for a Bustard.

Legs rather short. *Male* has a black ruff and white crest, with black tip. Of moderate size.

837. Houbara macqueeni. THE HOUBARA BUSTARD.

In honour of the sender of the specimens described by J. E. Gray.
Houbara, Tilaor, *Punjab*; **Taloor,** *Sind.*

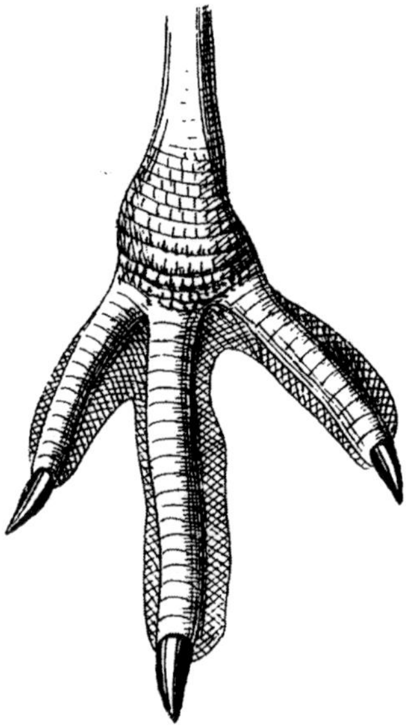

♂ 28″ to 30″; 4 to $5\frac{1}{4}$ lbs. ♀ 25″ to $27\frac{1}{2}$″; 3 to $3\frac{3}{4}$ lbs. Legs green-yellow. Bill slate. Sexes alike. Plumage pale buff, pencilled black. Tail with bluish bands and lateral feathers, tipped cream-white. Primaries white base, black end.

Genus SYPHEOTIS.

συφεός = a hogsty; ὠτίς = a kind of Bustard.

Male with white wing and black plumage. Highly crested or with ear-tufts.—*Females* bigger than males.

838. Sypheotis bengalensis. THE BENGAL FLORIKIN.

Charas, *N. W. P.*; **Dabar,** *Nepal*; **Ooloo Moora,** *Assam.*

♂ 26″ to 27″; $3\frac{1}{2}$ to $4\frac{1}{4}$ lbs. ♀ 28″ to 29″; 4 to 5 lbs. Legs pale yellow. Bill dusky and yellow. Full breast-tuft. Above blue-buff, minutely mottled with black. Below deep glossy black.—*Female* fulvous, with black and brown mottlings. Neck with dark lines.

839. Sypheotis auritus. THE LIKH OR LESSER FLORIKIN.

Kurmor, *Guzerat*; **Tun-mor,** *Deccan*; **Chini-mor,** *Belgaom*; **Likh,** *N. W. P.*; **Charas,** *S. India*; **Kannoul** (Canarese).

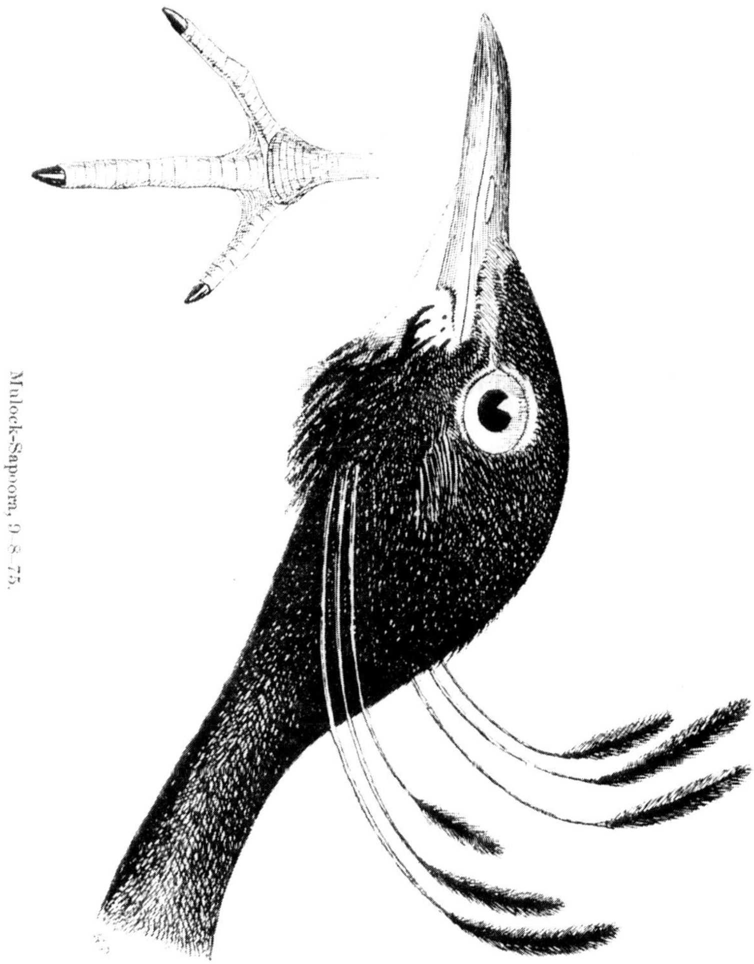

♂ $17\frac{1}{4}''$ to $19''$; 14 to 20 oz. ♀ $18''$ to $21''$; 18 to 24 oz. Legs whitish yellow. Bill dusky and yellow. Chin white. Primaries sharp-pointed. Base of feathers rose-colour.—*Female* clouded and barred deep brown.

Family CURSORIDÆ. Courier-Plovers.

Resemble Bustards in anatomy, but they are of small size and do not change plumage at breeding-season. One species, ***Cursorius pluvianus***, peculiar to N. Africa, and one species, *C. oreophilus*, in Chili and Falkland Isles.

Bill somewhat slender. Three toes only. Plumage brown and rufous.

Genus CURSORIUS.

Cursōrius = pertaining to a race-course; *cursor* = a runner, from *curro* = I run.

Nostrils not in a groove. Tail short, of 12 feathers. First and second quills longest. Lateral toes divided.

Cursorius gallicus. The Cream-coloured or European Courier-Plover.

Gallicus = of the Gauls, *Galli*. Gmelin seems to have thought it only occurred in France.

♂ 10″. Legs cream. Bill brown, tip black. Irides pale grey.—*Male*: Forehead pale buff, hinder part shading into grey, below which is a triangular black spot. Wing-coverts cream-yellow. Crown pale orange.

Inhabits desert plains of W. Asia and N. Africa, being an occasional visitor to S. Europe, and a rare straggler to England in late autumn.

840. Cursorius coromandelicus. The Indian Courier-Plover.

Nukri (Hindi); **Yerra Chitawa** (Telugu).

♂ 9″ to 10″. Legs cream-white. Bill black. Irides brown. Black from eye to nape. White eyebrow. Abdomen chestnut, with black bar. Crown bright red.

Genus RHINOPTILUS.

ρίν = a nose.

Adopted by Jerdon as a mountain-form of *Cursorius*. The form combines large eye and somewhat the colour of some of the true Plovers, with legs and general structure of Couriers. The species also exists in Africa.

Second and third primaries subequal and longest. Outer toe joined by web.

841. Rhinoptilus bitorquatus. THE DOUBLE-BANDED COURIER-PLOVER.

Adavi-wula-titti (Telugu).

♂ 9″ to 10″. Legs pale flesh-yellow. Bill yellow at base. Throat white, with red band. Broad brown gorget and second white collar. First and second quills obliquely marked. Crown black.

Family GLAREOLIDÆ. SWALLOW-PLOVERS OR PRATINCOLES.

Bill short and arched. Small hind toe. Gape very large. Tail semi-forked.

Inhabit S. and C. Europe, Asia, and as far E. as India and Africa, and as far S. as Natal. In anatomy allied to the Plovers. Linnæus placed them with Swallows, and Blyth approximates them to Night-Jars. Called "Sea-Partridges" by the French.

Genus **GLAREOLA.**

Glārĕŏla = a diminutive from *glārĕa* = gravel, from its haunting gravelly places.

Wings narrow, long, and pointed. Nostrils basal, oblique, semi-tubular.

(i.) *Tail forked.*

842. Glareola orientalis. THE LARGE SWALLOW-PLOVER.

♂ 10″. Legs dusky black. Bill black. Chin and throat rufous, bounded by black line from gape. Exterior tail-feathers project 1″ beyond central ones.—*Young* pale fulvous.

Glareola pratincola. THE COLLARED OR AUSTRALIAN PRATINCOLE.

Prātincŏla, from *prātum* = a meadow; *incŏla* = an inhabitant. From its frequenting the open meadows in Austria.

♂ 8⅘″ to 9½″. Legs brownish. Bill black. White tipping to short secondaries conspicuous. Exterior tail-feathers project 2″ to 2½″ beyond central ones. (S. F. ii. 284.)

(ii.) *Short and even tail.*

843. Glareola lactea. THE SMALL SWALLOW-PLOVER.

Utteran, *Sind.*

♂ 6½″. Legs dusky green. Bill black. Primaries brown, with first four white-shafted.

Glareola pratincola. Mandi Hissar, 21-4-79.

Family CHARADRIIDÆ. Plovers, Lapwings, and Stone-Curlews.

Comprising the true Plovers (Golden and Ringed, Lapwings, and Stone-Plovers). The first grade into the Courier-Plovers through the Dotterel, *Eudromias morinellus,* which species is not found out of the W. Palæarctic region (where it is widely distributed), except in winter, when it migrates to N. Africa.

Bill short, basal half soft. Long nasal groove. Wings long and pointed. Gape small. Hind toe generally wanting.

Subfamily Charadriinæ.

Bill short, slightly enlarged on top at tip. First quill usually longest.

Genus **SQUATAROLA.**

Squatărŏla = the Italian name; of uncertain origin.

Minute hind toe, with rudimentary claw.

844. Squatarola helvetica. The Grey Plover.

Swiss, from *Helvetii* = the inhabitants of Switzerland, whence M. de Réaumur first received specimens.

Barabattan, *India.*

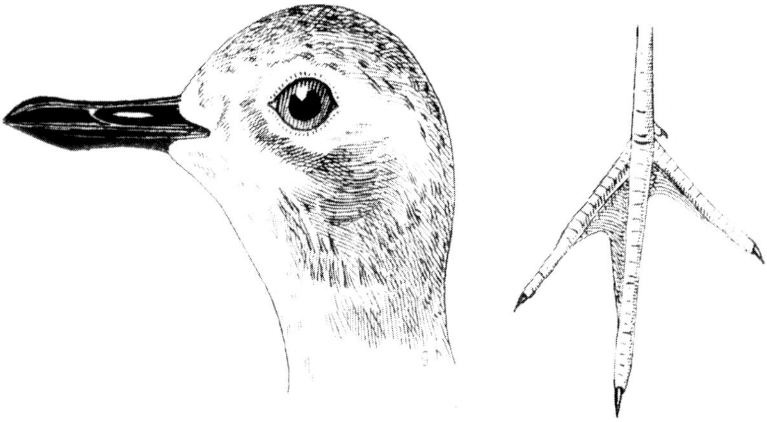

Kurrachee, 12–10–74.

♂ 12″. Legs black-grey. Bill black.—*In winter*: Forehead and chin white. Below white, with brown spots. Above brown, tipped white. *Axillaries black.*—*In summer*: Lower surface deep black, edged white. Back barred black and white.

Genus CHARADRIUS.

Charădrius = χαραδριός, in classical Greek, a bird dwelling in clefts or river-valleys, χαράδραι. The sight of it was held to be a cure for jaundice.

No hind toe. Plumage brown, spotted yellow.

Charadrius pluvialis. The European Golden Plover.

Pluviālis = rainy; from *plŭvia* = rain. Charleton says because it frequents places damp from rain, and marshes. Littré derives the French *pluvier* from the fact of the birds only reaching France in the rainy season.

♂ 7⅘″. Legs blue-grey. Bill black.—*In winter*: Above black, mottled golden. Throat, lower breast, and abdomen pure white. *Axillaries pure white.*—*In summer*: Above black, mottled golden and white. Throat, breast, and belly black. (S. F. vii. 186.)

Reigns in the W. Palæarctic, and *C. virginicus* in the Nearctic region.

Charadrius fulvus. THE EASTERN GOLDEN PLOVER.

Fulvus = tawny.
Chota battan, *India.*

♂ 10″. ♀ 9½″. Legs plumbeous green. Bill black.—*In winter*: Above dull grey, with triangular spots. Breast white, spotted yellow. Primaries black. *Axillaries smoky grey.*—*In summer*: Above darker, and spots smaller. Beneath deep black, edged white.

Breeds in E. Siberia, and has a wide range in Asia and Australia, but it rarely reaches Europe.

Genus ÆGIALITIS.

αἰγιαλῖτις = of the shore, *αἰγιᾰλός*.

The Sand-Plovers, found throughout the temperate parts of the Palæarctic region, wintering in Africa, India, and S. China. There are many species of Ringed Plovers in America, Africa, and Australia.

No hind toe. Of small size. Often with black collar. Sexes alike.

(i.) *Of stouter form and shorter tail. More or less rufous on neck and throat. Shafts of all but first white. Frequent the shore.*

Ægialitis vereda.

♂ 8¼″. Legs yellowish. Bill black.—*In winter*: More or less buffy below. Undertail white. Shafts of first and second primaries white. *Axillaries dark grey.*—*In summer*: Crown and above hair-brown. Forehead, eyelids, and chin white. Collar buff. Broad rufous breast-band. (S. F. i. 83.)

Ægialitis asiatica.

♂ 7½″. Legs horn. Bill black.—*In winter*: Crown, nape, and above hair-brown. Broad rufous breast-band. *Axillaries white.*—*In summer*: Above pale brown. No breast-band, but patch dusky grey on each side of breast. (S. F. vii. 438.)

846. Ægialitis geoffroyi. THE LARGE SAND-PLOVER.

♂ 8½″ to 9¼″; 2½ to 3 oz. Legs grey-green. Bill black.—*In winter*: Grey-brown. Eye-streak and above bill white. Below white. Secondaries partly white on outer web. Shafts of all primaries white.—*In summer*: White mark on each side of black forehead. Breast rufous. Throat white.

847. Ægialitis mongola. The Lesser Sand-Plover.

♂ $7\frac{1}{4}''$ to $8''$. Legs plumbeous. Bill black.
Similar to last, but smaller.

848. Ægialitis cantiana. The Kentish Ringed Plover.

Cantiāna = Kentish, because specimens were first sent to Latham by Dr. Boys from Sandwich, in Kent.

♂ $6\frac{1}{2}''$ to $6\frac{3}{4}''$; $1\frac{1}{4}$ to $1\frac{1}{3}$ oz. Legs dusky grey. Bill black. Large patch black on each side of breast. Central tail ashy.

Ægialitis placida.

Greyish fuscous. Quills fuscous black. Front, throat, collar, below and margins of wing-coverts white. Black and grey breast-band.

(ii.) *Of smaller size, with black collar and frontal band. Shafts of all primaries but first brown. Frequent plains and dry river-beds.*

849. Ægialitis dubia. The Indian Ringed Plover.

Zinea, *India*; **Bytu-ulanka** (Telugu).

♂ $7\frac{1}{4}''$. Legs yellow. Bill black, base yellow. Frontal zone yellow. Band from top of head, through eye and ear-coverts, black. White collar, with black border narrowing behind.

850. Ægialitis minuta. THE LESSER RINGED PLOVER.

Mandi Hissar, 22-4-79.

♂ $6\frac{1}{2}''$. Legs yellow. Bill black, base yellow.
Similar to last, but smaller.

Ægialitis nigrifrons.

♂ $6\frac{1}{2}''$. Legs orange-yellow. Bill yellow, tip black. Forehead, streak on either side extending through eye and ear and meeting behind, dark brown. Breast-band brown-black. Wing-coverts ashy. Scapulars maroon.

Subfamily VANELLINÆ. LAPWINGS.

Some with crests, with spurred wings, and with wattles. Plumage in masses. Dark band usually on white tail.

(i.) *Four toes. Wing not spurred. Generally no wattles about bill.*

Genus **VANELLUS.**

Formerly often spelt *Vannellus,* diminutive of *vannus* = a fan, whence the French name *Vanneau.*

Head crested. Fourth and fifth quills longest. Tubercle on wing. Very short hind toe. Breeds in Punjab.

851. Vanellus vulgaris. THE PEEWIT OR CRESTED LAPWING.

Vulgāris = common, from *vulgus* = the multitude.

♂ $12''$. Legs orange-brown. Bill black. Black slender crest. Above green, glossed purple. Abdomen white. Undertail chestnut.—*In winter*: Chin and throat white.

Genus CHETTUSIA.

Head not crested. Plumage ashy.

Found in Europe, Asia, Africa, and West-India isles.

852. Chettusia gregaria. The Black-sided Lapwing.

♂ 13″. Legs dull black. Bill black. Crown black. Abdomen deep black, bordered chestnut.—*In winter*: Crown olive. No abdominal patch.

853. Chettusia leucura. The White-tailed Lapwing.

λευκός = white.

♂ 11″. Legs bright yellow. Bill black. Belly and flanks tinged rosy.

854. Chettusia inornata. The Grey-headed Lapwing.

Chappour, *India.*

♂ 15″. Legs bright yellow. Bill black. Head, neck, and breast light grey, passing into black.

(ii.) *Four toes. Flesh wattles at base of bill.*

Genus LOBIVANELLUS.

With wattles at base of bill. Small hind toe.

855. Lobivanellus indicus. The Red-wattled Lapwing.

Titai, Titiri, *India*; **Yennapa, Chittawa** (Telugu); **Alkati** (Tamil).

♂ 13″. Legs bright yellow. Bill red, tip black. Head and breast black. Side of neck and round nape white.

Lobivanellus atronuchalis. THE BURMESE RED-WATTLED LAPWING.

White ear-patch does not extend round the nape.

Genus SARCIOPHORUS.

σαρκιόν = a little bit of flesh; φορέω = I carry.

With wattles at base of bill. No hind toe.

856. Sarciophorus malabaricus. THE YELLOW-WATTLED LAPWING.

Zirdo, *India*; **Chitawa** (Telugu); **Jithiri**, *N.W.P.*; **Alkati** (Tamil).

♂ 12″. Legs yellow. Bill yellow, black tip. Chin, throat, breast, and upper plumage pale ashy.

(iii.) *Some with only three toes. Strong spines on shoulder of wing.*

Genus HOPLOPTERUS.

No hind toe. Wing with horny spur.
Found in Africa, Asia, and South America.

857. Hoplopterus ventralis. THE SPUR-WINGED LAPWING.

Ventrālis, adj. = a belly-band.

♂ 12″. Legs red-black. Bill black. Head, crest, and broad band down throat black. Abdomen white, with broken black band.

Subfamily ESACINÆ. STONE-CURLEW.

Bill strong, dilated above and below. Nail of middle toe hollowed beneath.

According to last results these are BUSTARDS and not PLOVERS.

Genus ESACUS.

Edges of bill notched towards tip.
Found in India, Indian Archipelago, and Australia.

858. Esacus recurvirostris. THE LARGE STONE-CURLEW.

Abi, Bara Karwanak, *India*; **Talur**, *Sind*; **Gang-titai**, *Bengal.*

♂ 19″ to 21″; 1¾ lbs. Legs yellow. Bill yellow, tip black. Eyebrow, ear-coverts, and moustache blackish. Plumage above grey. Below white.

Esacus magnirostris. THE AUSTRALIAN STONE-CURLEW.

♂ 22½″. Legs yellow. Bill greenish. Band round eye extending back over ear-coverts. Chin and throat pure white. Nape, back, and scapulars earth-brown. First five primaries umber-brown. (S. F. ii. 290.)

Genus **ŒDICNEMUS.**

οἶδος = a swelling; *κνήμη* = a leg.

Plumage brown and striated. Eye large. Nostrils in long groove. Migratory, inhabiting all parts except North America.

859. Œdicnemus indicus. THE GOGGLE-EYE OR BASTARD FLORIKIN, OR ENGLISH STONE-CURLEW.

Karwanak, Barsiri, Lambi, *India*; **Kharma,** *Bengal*; **Kalleydu** (Telugu); **Kana mosal** (Tamil).

♂ 16″ to 17″; ¾ lb. Legs yellow. Bill yellow, black tip. Upper

Laughton Loharilung, 29–8–75.

feathers red-ashy, with longitudinal stripe. Breast reddish, with fine streaks.

Family HÆMATOPODIDÆ. SEA-PLOVERS.

Small hind toe raised above the others. Plumage variegated.

Chiefly sea-shore birds, distributed all over the world. And here Bonaparte puts the Turnstones and Crab-Plovers in one family, while Gray groups them with Plovers.

Subfamily STREPSILINÆ.

Upper mandible turns up slightly.

Genus **STREPSILAS.**

Strepsīlas, from στρέφω = I turn, and λᾶας, contracted in Attic to λᾶς = a stone.

Top of bill compressed and truncated.

860. Strepsilas interpres. THE TURNSTONE.

Interprĕs = an agent between two parties, an explainer; from *inter* = between, and the root of the Sanskrit *prath* = unfold (whence πλατύς = broad); perhaps in allusion to its warning note.

♂ $8\frac{1}{2}''$ to $9\frac{1}{2}''$; $3\frac{1}{2}$ to 4 oz. Legs orange-yellow. Bill black. Sexes

Kurrachee, 21-6-75.

alike. Crown white, with black stripes. Black stripe from eye meets another from mouth behind eye. Incomplete collar with gorget, and a second incomplete band towards wing-shoulder.—*In winter*: Below pure white. Crown hair-brown. Gape-line mottled.

Found in most parts of the world.

Subfamily DROMADINÆ.

Bill long, arching towards tip; strongly angulated below.

Genus **DROMAS**.

δρομάς = a street-walker, a runner.

Feet much webbed.

Found in India. A remarkable genus.

861. **Dromas ardeola.** THE CRAB-PLOVER.

♂ 15″. Legs plumbeous. Bill black. Head, neck, and below white. Mantle and wing-coverts black.

Subfamily HÆMATOPODINÆ.

Bill long, strong, and truncated. Plumage black or pied.

Genus **HÆMATOPUS**.

Hæmătŏpus = with blood-coloured feet; from *αἷμα* = blood; *πούς* = a foot.

Bill slightly bent up. Bony toes.

Found in most parts. Several species in America.

862. **Hæmatopus ostralegus.** THE OYSTER-CATCHER.

Ostrĕa = an oyster; *lĕgo* = I bring together, collect.

Darya gajpaon, *India*; **Yerri kali ulanka** (Telugu).

♂ 16″. Legs pink-red. Bill orange-yellow. Head, neck, back, wings, and tail black; rest white. Broad wing-band.—*Young* birds less black; feathers pale-edged.

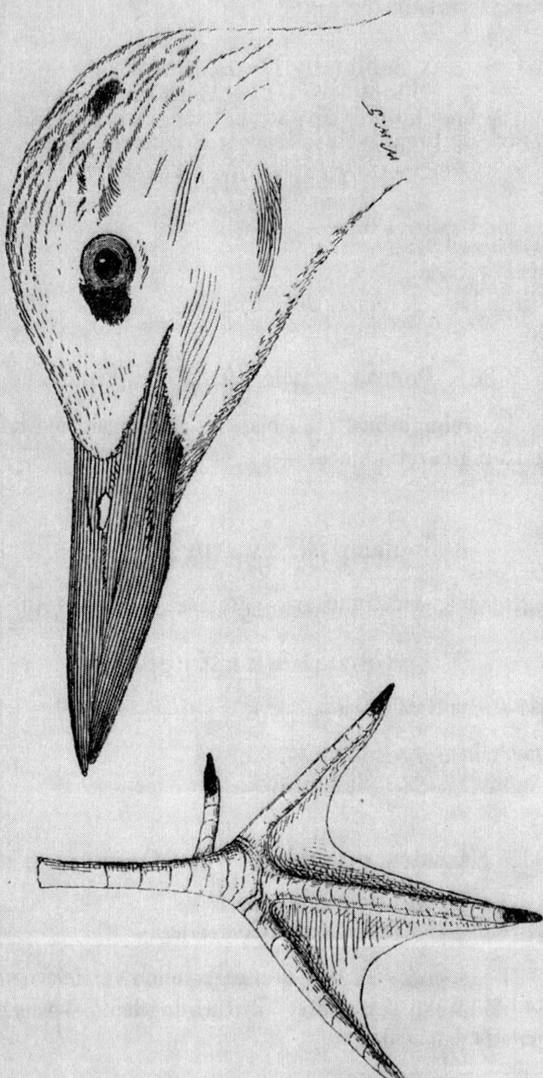

861. *Dromas ardeola.* Babur Island, 22–10–75.

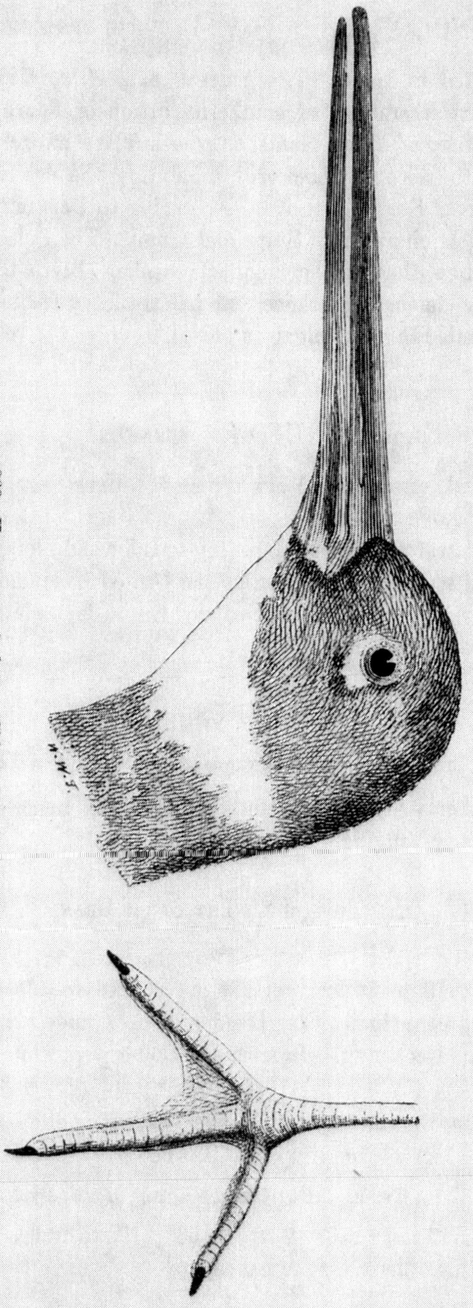

862. *Hæmatopus ostralegus.* Chinmee Creek, 23–10–75.

Family THINOCORIDÆ. GAME-PLOVERS OR SHORE-LARKS.

Not represented in India. Two genera: one, *Attagis*, in Falkland Isles and on lofty mountains of southern portion of South America, within the boundary of Alpine plants, or even in places entirely destitute of vegetation; the second, *Thinocorus*, inhabiting the desolate valleys of southern parts of South America. According to Darwin these birds partake both of the character of Snipe and Quail. Their character and mode of flight show them to be modified Grallæ. Blyth thinks they approach Pteroclidæ in appearance and habit. They frequent upland plains, and resemble the Ptarmigan in habits.

Family GRUIDÆ. CRANES.

Bill short, stout, straight, and slightly cleft. Large size. Plumage grey on white. Long neck.

Inhabit the Palæarctic region, migrating to India and North Africa in winter. A rare straggler to portion of the United Kingdom, probably from Scandinavia. Externally allied to Bustards; while internal anatomy is more that of Plovers.

Genus GRUS.

Grus = a Crane, in classical Latin; akin to γέρἄνος, *gallus*, *garrio* = I chatter, &c.

Base of bill, orbits, and sometimes whole head nude. Tertiaries lengthened and overhanging.

863. Grus antigone. THE SARUS CRANE.

Sirhaus (Hindi); **Sarus, Gyogya**, *Arakan.*

♂ 56″ to 60″; 16 to 20 lbs. ♀ 53″ to 55″; 15 to 17½ lbs. Legs rose-red. Bill green, tip brown. Head and neck nude, crimson, with few black hairs. Neck-ring.—*In summer*: Collar pure white.

864. Grus leucogeranus. THE LARGE WHITE, OR SNOW-WREATH, OR SIBERIAN CRANE.

Karekhur, *N. W. P.*; **Tunhi**, *Oudh*; **Chini Kalung**, *Hansi*; **Syakbal**, *Cubul.*

♂ 52″ to 56″; 16 to 19 lbs. ♀ 48″ to 53″; 12½ to 16 lbs. Legs red. Bill umber. Quills black. Face naked, red.

865. Grus communis. THE COMMON CRANE.

Kooroonch, Koorch, *N. W. P.*; **Kul-lung,** *Upper India*; **Kallam,** *Deccan*; **Kulungi** (Telugu); **Wainu,** *Manipur.*

♂ 43″ to 48″; 9½ to 13 lbs. Legs dull black. Bill green, tip dark. Forehead nude, with black hairs. Crown nude, orange; between eyes white. Plumage ashy blue.—*Young* birds want the naked patch.

Genus ANTHROPOIDES.

ἀνθρποειδής = in the shape of a man.

Head and neck densely feathered. Neck and breast-feathers lanceolate and hackled.

866. Anthropoides virgo. THE DEMOISELLE CRANE.

Virgo = a maiden, from the bird's elegant appearance and dancing propensity.

Karkarra, *N. W. P.*; **Ghanto,** *Nepal*; **Kurkurchi,** *Sattara*; **Parouthakee,** *Mysore*; **Wadakoraka** (Telugu); **Shuck duruck,** *Cabul.*

♂ 31″ to 36″; 5 to 6¾ lbs. Legs black. Bill green, tip pink. Face, neck, and breast-plumes black. Eye-tuft of white decomposed feathers.—*Young* birds have no black and want ear-tuft.

Tribe *LONGIROSTRES.*

Longus = long; *rostrum* = a bill.

Bill long and slender. Hallux short or raised. Exterior toe generally joined to middle by web.

Family SCOLOPACIDÆ.

Bill long, slender and soft. Wings long. Tail short. Plumage brown above, white or ashy beneath. Hind toe generally elevated.

Subfamily SCOLOPACINÆ.

Bill long and straight, rather soft, swollen and bent over at tip. Eyes set far back. Plumage rich, often streaked black and yellow.

Genus SCOLOPAX.

Scŏlŏpax = σκολόπαξ, a kind of Snipe mentioned by Aristotle; probably from σκόλοψ = a thing pointed, a stake, and akin to σκάλλω = I stir up, probe, &c.

Tibia plumed to joint. Tail of 12 uniform feathers.

867. Scolopax rusticola. The Common Woodcock.

Rusticŏla = a little Heath-cock in Pliny; *rusticŭlus* = a little countryman in Cicero. Diminutive of *rusticus* = of or belonging to the country, *rus*.

Sim-titar, Kumattu, Chinjarol, *Chamba*; **Kangtruk,** *Manipur*; **Wilate-chaha,** *Chittagong*; **Murgh-i-zerak,** *Persia*.

♂ 13″ to 15″; 9 to 14 oz. ♀ 16″. Legs livid. Bill 3″, flesh-grey. Four cross-bars on head. Plumage variegated brown, yellow, and grey, with black lines and spots.—*Female* not so bright.

Woodcock are scattered throughout the world. A winter visitant to India. There are other true Woodcock: one in Java (*S. saturata*), and one (*S. minor*) in Eastern United States of America.

Genus GALLINAGO.

From *gallina* = a hen, feminine of an obsolete adjective *gallinus*, from *gallus* = a cock. The termination is adjectival, as if from *gallinax*, like *virago* from *virax*.

Tibia bare for small space. Tail of 16 to 28 feathers.

Scattered all over the world, and breeds in northern parts of Europe and Asia.

(i.) *Tail of* 16 *or* 18 *feathers, four on each side, attenuated and stiff.*

868. Gallinago nemoricola. The Wood-Snipe.

Ban-chaha, *Nepal*.

♂ 11½″ to 12½″; 5 to 6 oz. ♀ 13″; 7 oz. Legs green. Bill 2¾″, red-brown. Top of head and back black, marked rufous grey. Breast ashy. Outer margin of first three primaries nearly uniform with rest of feathers. Abdomen, vent, and lower tail-coverts closely barred.

Home in the Himalayas.

(ii.) *Tail of* 20 *to* 28 *feathers. Laterals* 5 *to* 10 *on each side attenuated and stiff.*

869. Gallinago solitaria. The Eastern or Solitary Snipe.

Bharka, *Nepal*.

♂ 12″ to 13″; 5 to 8 oz. ♀ 13″; 9 oz. Legs green. Bill 2¾″, red-brown. Pale buff stripe along scapular and inner edge of wing. Breast olive, dashed white. Outer margins of first three primaries white. Abdomen, vent, and lower tail-coverts unbarred.—*Female* darker.

Home in the Himalayas.

870. Gallinago stenura. THE PINTAIL SNIPE.

Chaha, *N.W.P.*; **Bharka,** *Nepal*; **Chegga,** *Lower Bengal*; **Cherayga,** *Assam*; **Cheklonbi,** *Manipur*; **Tibud,** *Ratnagiri*; **Oolan,** *S. India*; **Birku,** *Malaya*; **Kaswatua,** *Ceylon.*

♂ $9\frac{3}{4}''$ to $10''$; 4 to 5 oz. ♀ $10''$ to $11\frac{1}{4}''$. Legs grey-green. Bill

$2\frac{1}{2}''$, red-brown. Under wing-coverts richly barred dusky and white. Six pin-feathers on each side of tail.

Breeds far north in Siberia.

(iii.) *Tail of* 14 *to* 16 *feathers, of same width.*

871. Gallinago cælestis. THE FANTAIL OR COMMON SNIPE.

Cælestis = pertaining to or coming from heaven, *cælum*. The Snipe was called by the older authors *Capella cælestis,* from its imitating the voice of a goat (*capella*) in its "drumming" during the breeding-season.

Chaha, *N. W. P.*; **Bharka,** *Nepal*; **Chegga,** *Lower Bengal*; **Cheryga,** *Assam*; **Chek lonbli,** *Manipur*; **Tibud,** *Ratnagiri*; **Oolan,** *S. India*; **Kadakecho,** *Orissa*; **Ketbatta,** *Ceylon*; **Pashalek,** *Afghanistan*; **Mahalamche,** *Yarkand.*

♂ $9''$ to $11\frac{1}{3}''$; $3\frac{3}{4}$ to 5 oz. ♀ $9''$ to $12\frac{1}{2}''$; 3 to $5\frac{1}{2}$ oz. Legs green-drab. Bill $2\frac{3}{4}''$, red-brown. Back velvet-black, crossed chestnut with streaks of yellow. Lower wing-coverts faintly barred.—*Female* the same. Eminently gregarious.

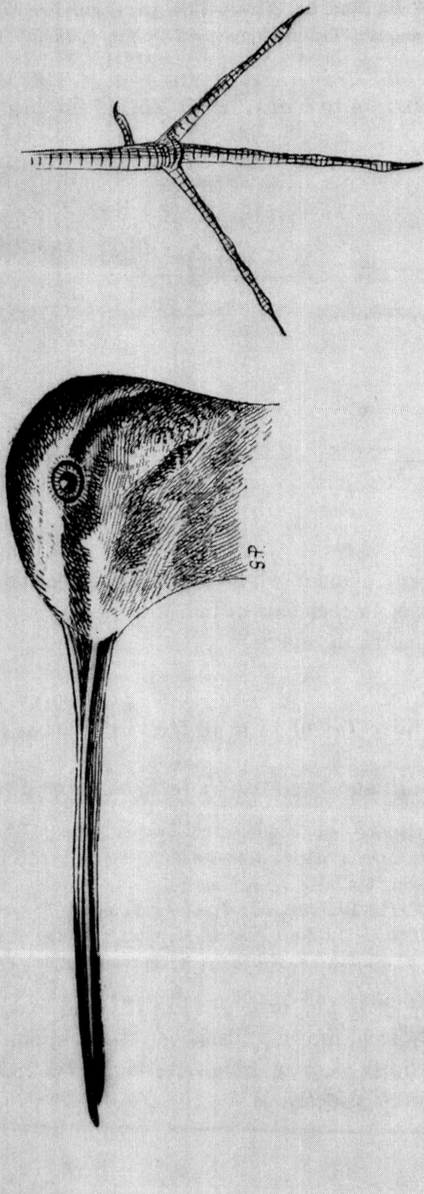

871. *Gallinago cælestis.*

(iv.) *Tail of* 12 *uniform feathers.*

872. Gallinago gallinula. The Jack Snipe.

Gallinŭla = a chicken; diminutive of *gallina* = a hen.
Chota bharka, *Nepal*; **Oolan,** *Madras*; **Tibud,** *Ratnagiri.*

♂ $7\frac{3}{4}''$ to $9''$; $1\frac{1}{2}$ to $2\frac{1}{2}$ oz. ♀ $8\frac{1}{2}''$. Legs green-grey. Bill $1\frac{1}{2}''$ to $1\frac{3}{4}''$, blackish. Back black, glossed green. Two yellow bands from shoulder to tail.

Occur in Asia Minor, Palestine, N. Africa, Mediterranean, and Europe, excluding Atlantic isles, Faroes, and Iceland. A winter visitant to India, summering and breeding north of 60° N. latitude to far within Arctic circle.

Genus RHYNCHÆA.

ῥύγχος = a beak.

Tibia much denuded. Bill curved slightly down at tip. Tail of 14 to 16 feathers.

873. Rhynchæa bengalensis. The Painted Snipe.

Ohari, *Nepal*; **Kone,** *Singbhoom*; **Tibud,** *Ratnagiri*; **Mail-ulan,** *Madras*; **Baggerjee,** *Lower Bengal.*

♂ $9\frac{1}{4}''$ to $10''$; $3\frac{1}{2}$ to 5 oz. ♀ $9\frac{3}{4}''$ to $11''$; $4\frac{1}{2}$ to $6\frac{1}{2}$ oz. Legs green. Bill $1\frac{7}{8}''$, red-brown. Line on head and one from eye to nape buff. Quills with outer webs spotted.—*Female*: Darker face. Neck chestnut.

Extends to Sumatra, Java, Borneo, and Philippines.

Subfamily LIMOSINÆ. GODWITS.

Bill lengthened, straight, or bent upwards. Plain plumage. Web between outer toes. Eyes less remote. Like SNIPES in bill, and like STINTS in plumage.

Scattered all over the world. Two or three species recorded from Australia and New Zealand, and two from America.

Genus **MACRORHAMPHUS.**

With a long beak; from *μακρός* + *ῥάμφος*.

Bill more high than wide. Feet partly webbed.

874. Macrorhamphus semipalmatus. THE SNIPE-BILLED GODWIT.

♂ 13¼″ to 13½″; 4 oz. ♀ 13″ to 13¾″. Legs green. Bill 2⅞″, dusky.—*In winter*: Ash-brown. Central tail-feathers spotted on outer web.—*In summer*: Rufous. Wing brown, edged white. Tail banded black and white.

Genus **PSEUDOTOTANUS.**

Bill longer than head, stout, nearly straight, but culmen recurved.

Pseudototanus haughtoni. ARMSTRONG'S YELLOWSHANKS.

♂ 12″ to 13″; 3⅛ oz. ♀ 13″. Legs ochreous. Bill plumbeous. Broad stripe from forehead. Chin, neck, breast, abdomen, and wing-lining white. Crown, neck, secondaries, and tertiaries pale ashy.

Genus **LIMOSA.**

Limōsus = muddy, from *limus* = mud.

Bill cylindrical at base, obtuse at tip. Nail of middle toe dilated internally.

875. Limosa ægocephala. THE BLACK-TAILED GODWIT.

The Linnean form of *αἰγοκέφαλος*, a bird mentioned by Aristotle; from *αἴξ* = a goat, and *κεφαλή* = the head.

Goodera, Gairiya, *N. W. P.*; **Malgujha,** *Nepal*; **Jaurali,** *Bengal*; **Susling,** *Sind*; **Tonda ulanka** (Telugu).

♂ 16″ to 18″; 8 to 12 oz. ♀ 18″ to 21″; 9 to 15 oz. Legs dusky. Bill 3½″ to 5″, fleshy.—*In winter*: Above ash-brown. Below grey-white.—*In summer*: Back black, tipped red. Breast red. Abdomen white.

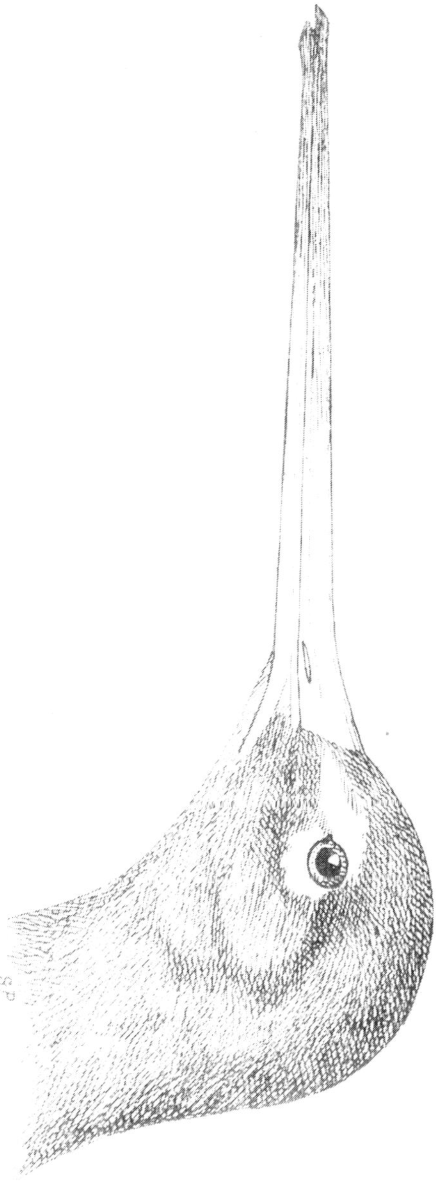

875. *Limosa ægocephala.*

Limosa lapponica. THE BAR-TAILED GODWIT.

Lappōnica = of Lapland.

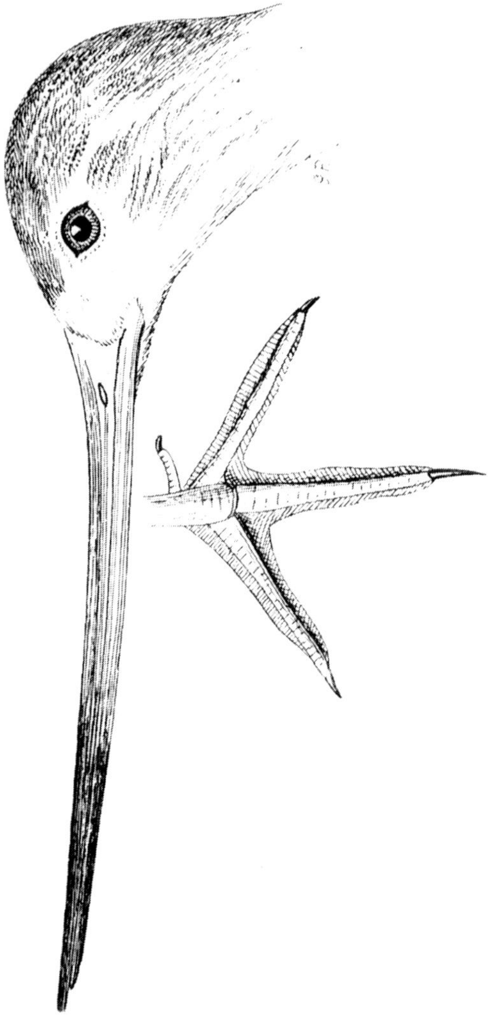

Kurrachee, 29-10-76.

♂ $13\frac{1}{2}''$ to $14\frac{3}{4}''$; $7\frac{1}{2}$ to 10 oz. ♀ $15\frac{3}{4}''$; 9 to $11\frac{1}{3}$ oz. Legs black. Bill $3''$ to $3\frac{1}{2}''$, pink and black.—*In winter*: Above earthy, and dark central shaft.—*In summer*: Below pale red. Above black-brown, marbled grey. (S. F. i. 235.)

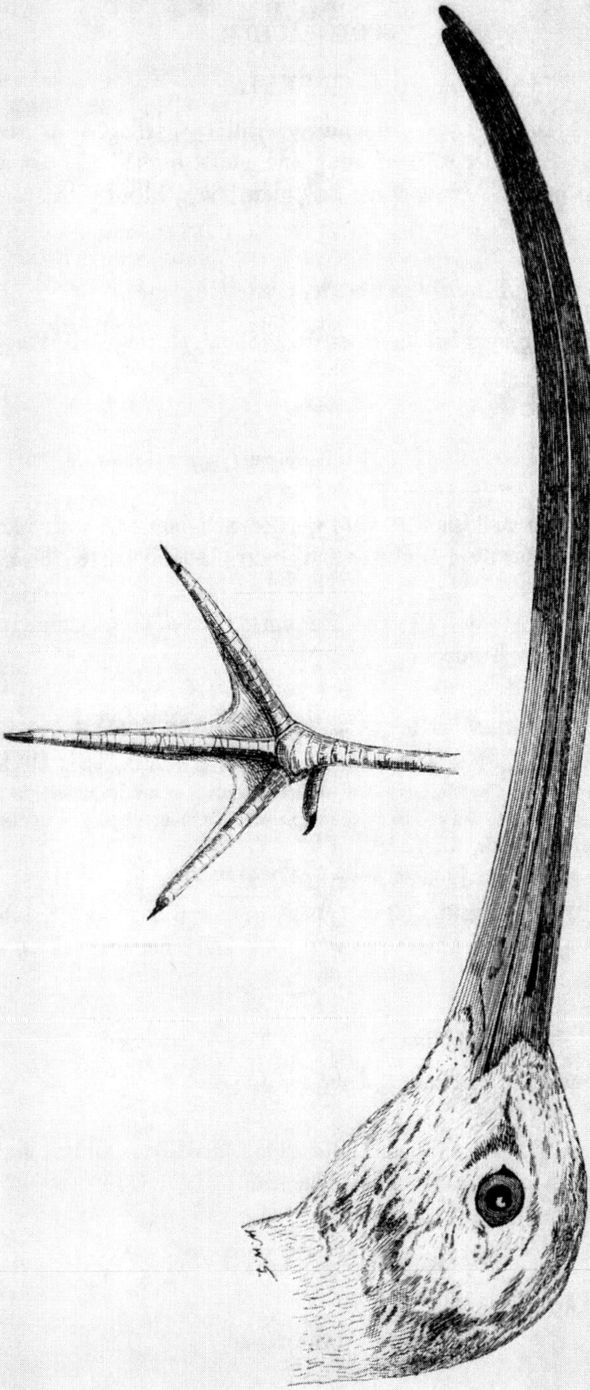

87. *Numenius arquata.*

Genus TEREKIA.

♂ 9″. ♀ 10½″. Legs pale orange. Bill 1⅘″, orange.—*In winter*: Ashy blue. Shoulder-edge of wing and quills brown. Breast ashy, with streaks of red.—*In summer*: Scapulars black, edged with brown.

Subfamily NUMENINÆ. CURLEWS.

Bill very long, curved downwards. Same plumage all the year round.

Genus NUMENIUS.

Nūmēnius = νουμήνιος, a kind of Curlew in Diogenes Laërtius (about A.D. 200); from νέος = new, and μήνη = the moon, from its "crescent" beak.

Hind toe with nail short. Feet webbed and bordered with narrow membrane. Differ from GODWITS and STINTS in their curved beak and fixed plumage.

Migratory and found all over the world. Said to perch on trees occasionally in N. Europe.

877. Numenius arquata. THE COMMON CURLEW.

The mediæval name. It is generally said to be derived from the bird's bill being bent like a bow, *arcus*; but it more likely refers to *arquatus morbus* = the jaundice ("when the skin turns to the yellow colour of the rainbow"), in allusion to the legend about *Charadrius*, *Galbula*, *Icterus*, &c.

Goar, Goungh, *India*; **Choppa, Sada Kastachura,** *Bengal.*

♂ 21″; 27 oz. ♀ 26″; 30 oz. Legs grey. Bill 4″ to 7¼″, brown. Above brown, edged rufous. Lower back and abdomen white, with dusky spots.

878. Numenius phæopus. THE WHIMBREL.

The mediæval name; from φαιός = dusky, and πούς = a foot.

Chota, Goungh, *India.*

♂ 16″. ♀ 18″. Legs bluish. Bill 3″ to 3½″, dusky. Crown brown, with pale broad eye-streak. Flanks barred.

Genus IBIDORHYNCHUS.

ἶβις = Ibis; ῥύγχος = a bill.

No hind toe, and outer toe free or nearly so.

878. *Numenius phæopus.*—10-10-75.

879. Ibidorhynchus struthersi. The Red-billed Curlew.

♂ 16″; 10 oz. Legs blood-red. Bill $3\frac{3}{4}$″, crimson. Head black, mixed grey and margined white. Plumage olive.

Peculiar to Himalayas. Hodgson says it has the short legs and feet of a Plover. Gould remarks that its legs and feet are those of an Oyster-catcher, and its bill that of an Ibis.

Subfamily Tringinæ. Stints.

Bill moderate, soft, and occasionally dilated or curved. Wings long. Tail short. Toes usually divided to base or with rudimentary web.

Stints have shorter bills and legs than Godwits, and shorter and softer bills than Sandpipers. Change of plumage in summer darker above and rufous beneath. Frequent marine marshes and sea-shore. Retire north in summer.

It is on the shore, after recess of the tide, in company with other species, that these birds are seen collecting their food from the refuse of the ocean, or quietly and intently probing the moist sand for worms and small shell-fish, running before the advancing surf and profiting by what is left behind.

Genus PHILOMACHUS.

φιλέω = I love; μάχη = a fight.

Web only between outer and middle toe. Males much larger than females.

880. Philomachus pugnax. The Ruff.

Pugnax = fond of fighting; from *pugna* = a fight.
Geh-wala, *India.*

♂ 12″ to 13″; 6 oz. Legs yellow. Bill $1\frac{1}{3}$″, brown.—*In winter*: *Male* has upper plumage brown, with black spots. Lower parts white. *Female* smaller.—*In summer*: *Male* only has ruff.

Genus TRINGA.

The late Latin form of Aristotle's τρύγγας. Derivation unknown.

Bill channelled almost to the tip. Toes free or barely united by a web.

(i.) *Bill straight. Small web.*

881. Tringa canutus. The Knot.

In honour of King Canute, because it was supposed to come from Denmark; or perhaps from its littoral habits, in allusion to the story of Canute's celebrated reproof to his courtiers.

♂ 10″. Legs black. Bill $1\frac{1}{2}$″, bluish.—*In winter*: Ash-grey.—*In summer*: Above dark black, edged brown and white. Beneath chestnut.

(ii.) *Bill distinctly turned down at tip. Toes perfectly free.*

Tringa crassirostris. THE THICK-BILLED STINT.

♂ 11½″ to 12″. ♀ 11½″ to 12″. Legs dusky. Bill 1½″ to 2″, black. —*In winter*: Breast mottled, brown spots heart-shaped. Above ashy, tipped white.—*In summer*: Breast-feathers black, with white cross-band. (S. F. i. 240.)

882. Tringa subarquata. THE CURLEW STINT.

Subarquāta = a little like a Curlew, *Arquāta*.

♂ 8″ to 8¾″. Legs grey. Bill 1½″, black.—*In winter*: Face, throat, and beneath white. Brown streak from gape to eye.

883. Tringa cinclus. THE DUNLIN.

♂ 7½″. Bill 1¼″, black.—*In winter*: Ash-brown, shafts darker. Central tail dark brown. Laterals ashy, edged white. Abdomen white. —*In summer*: Head and abdomen black. Breast spotted white.

884. Tringa minuta. THE LITTLE STINT.

Chota pan loha, *India*.

♂ 6″. Legs black. Bill $\frac{7}{10}$″, black.—*In winter*: Above and sides ash-brown. Below white.—*In summer*: Head, above, and central tail black, edged rufous. Breast reddish. Shafts of primaries mostly white. Middle toe ⅔″.

Tringa damacensis

is like "*minuta.*" Shafts of primaries, with exception of first, brown. Middle toe 1″. (S. F. i. 244.)

Tringa albescens.

♂ 4″. ♀ 4⅕″. Legs blackish. Bill black. Forehead white. Primary shafts white about centre, sullied near base. Breast white.

885. Tringa temmincki. THE WHITE-TAILED STINT.

In honour of Coenraad Jacob Temminck, Keeper of the Leyden Museum, b. 1778, d. 1858.

♂ 6″ to 6¼″. Bill $\frac{7}{10}$″, black.—*In winter*: Above brown, with dusky streaks. Four central tail-feathers ash-brown. Laterals, throat, belly, and undertail pure white.

886. Tringa platyrhyncha. The Broad-billed Stint.

πλατύς = broad; ῥύγχος = a bill.

♂ 6¼″ to 7″. Legs dusky. Bill 1″ to 1⅓″, black. Sexes same size. Bill flat and slightly bent.—*In winter*: Above, tail, breast, and under-tail tinged rufous.—*In summer*: Above black, edged rufous. Black breast-spots.

Tringa sibirica. The Eastern Stint.

In summer: Crown and above broadly margined bright rufous. Upper throat unspotted. (S. F. v. 344.)

Genus EURINORHYNCHUS.

εὖ = well; ῥὶν = nose; ῥύγχος = a bill.

Bill with tip expanded. Toes well cleft. Small outer web.

887. Eurinorhynchus pygmæus. The Spoon-billed Stint.

♂ 6¼″. Legs black. Bill 1″, black. Forehead white. Tail-coverts dark. Shafts white, tipped black. Lower parts snow-white.

Genus CALIDRIS.

κάλιδρις or σκάλιδρις = a speckled water-bird in Aristotle. Derivation unknown.

No hind toe. Web very small.

888. Calidris arenaria. The Sanderling.

Arenāria = pertaining to sand, *arēna*.

27-10-75.

♂ 7½″ to 8″; 1¾ oz. Legs black. Bill 1″, black.—*In winter*: Ashy. Shafts brown. Head, edge of wing, and tail deep grey.—*In summer*: Head and cheeks black. Back, neck, and breast reddish, with black spots.

Subfamily PHALAROPINÆ. PHALAROPES or LOBEFOOTS.

Toes bordered by lobes. Plumage dense. Males incubate; female forsakes nest.

Inhabit north regions. Appearance in India occasional and accidental. Of dense plumage, said to swim and dive well. Yarrell classes them with Coots. Males alone incubate, females forsaking nest and leading a wandering life.

Genus **PHALAROPUS.**

Phalārŏpus, from φαλāρίς = a Coot, in classical Greek, which is from φάλāρος = having a patch of white (on its forehead); ποῦς = a foot.

Feet lobed.

(i.) *Bill broad.*

889. Phalaropus fulicarius. THE COMMON PHALAROPE.

Fŭlicārius = like a Coot, *fŭlica*.

♂ 8½″. ♀ 8″. Legs green. Bill ⅞″, red, tip brown.—*In winter*: Forehead and crown white. Grey nape-streak. White bar on wing. Beneath white.

(ii.) *Bill pointed.*

890. Phalaropus hyperboreus. THE LESSER PHALAROPE.

Hyperbŏrĕus = northern; ὑπερβόρεος = beyond Boreas, "at the back of the north wind;" from ὑπέρ = above, and βορέας = the north wind, the north.

♂ 6½″. Legs green. Bill ⅞″, dusky.—*In winter*: Crown brown. Back and tail brown, edged red.—*In summer*: Above black, edged red. Neck red.

Subfamily TOTANINÆ. SANDPIPERS.

Bill moderate, tip hard and pointed. Outer toe joined by web to middle one. Change of plumage in summer to black or dusky beneath, and not rufous.

Migratory birds scattered in both hemispheres. Winter visitants to India, breeding in North and Central Europe and Asia. They pick up small crustacea and molluscs from the surface, and do not insert their bills deeply like Snipes and Stints. Several are solitary in their habits.

Genus **ACTITIS.**

Bill long, straight, and grooved to tip. Slight change for summer plumage.

891. Actitis glareola. THE SPOTTED SANDPIPER.

Glārĕŏla, a diminutive from *glārĕa* = gravel, from its haunting gravelly places.
Chupka, Chobaha, *India*; **Chinna ulanka** (Telugu).

♂ $8\frac{1}{2}''$ to $9''$. Legs green. Bill $1\frac{1}{5}''$, green, tip black.—*In winter*: Forehead and above deep brown, with grey spots. Tail barred black and white; laterals white-spotted.—*In summer*: Back with black spots.

892. Actitis ochropus. THE GREEN SANDPIPER.

Ochrŏpus, from ὠχρός = pale yellow, and πούς = a foot.
Nella ulanka (Telugu).

♂ $9\frac{3}{4}''$ to $10\frac{1}{4}''$. Legs green. Bill $1\frac{1}{2}''$, green, tip black.—*In winter*: Above ashy, tinged green, with edging of small white spots. Tail, basal third white, rest white barred brown.—*In summer*: Darker, greener, and more spotted.

893. Actitis hypoleucos. THE COMMON SANDPIPER.

Hypoleucos = ὑπόλευκος, which generally = whitish (pale from the ordinary sense of ὑπό in composition, "somewhat"), but here plainly = white underneath. It was the bird's common mediæval name.
Potti ulanka (Telugu).

♂ $7\frac{3}{4}''$ to $8\frac{1}{4}''$. Legs pale green. Bill $1''$, dusky. In winter and summer the same. Above and four central tail-feathers glossed green, with cross brown lines. Quills, except first two, with spot on inner web.

893. *Actitis hypoleucos.*

Genus **TOTANUS.**

Totănus, Latinized from the Italian *Tótano.* Derivation unknown.

Bill distinctly curved, groove not extending to tip.

894. Totanus glottis. The Common Greenshanks.

γλῶττις = mouth of the windpipe.
Tim timma, *India*; **Gotra**, *Bengal.*

♂ 13″ to 15″. Legs greenish. Bill 2″ to $2\frac{1}{5}$″, dusky.—*In winter* and *summer* the same. Tail cross-barred and laterals white, with narrow streak on outer web. Head white, with brown streaks. Back brown, edged yellow.

895. Totanus stagnatilis. The Lesser Greenshanks.

Stăgnătilis = pertaining to ponds.
Chota gotra, *Bengal.*

♂ $10\frac{1}{2}$″. Legs pale green. Bill $1\frac{5}{8}$″, dusky.—*In winter*: Ash-brown. Quills brown, shafts white. Cheeks, neck, breast, and flanks spotted brown.—*In summer*: Beneath small, round, black spots.

896. Totanus fuscus. The Spotted Redshanks.

Fuscus = dusky.
Batan, *India*; **Yerra Kal ulanka** (Telugu).

♂ 13″; $7\frac{1}{4}$ to 9 oz. Legs orange-red. Bill $2\frac{1}{3}$″, orange, tip black. —*In winter*: Black patch near eye. Central tail ash-grey; outer tail vandyked white.—*In summer*: Vent and lower tail barred white and brown.

896. *Totanus fuscus.*

897. Totanus calidris. The Common Redshanks.

κάλιδρις or σκάλιδρις = a speckled water-bird, in Aristotle.
Chota battan, *India.*

♂ 10½″ to 11½″; 6 oz. Legs pale red. Bill 1¾″, red, tip dusky. Above brown. Darker shafts white and brown.

Known in flight by white on wing.

Family HIMANTOPIDÆ. STILTS and AVOCETS.

Bill very long and very thin, sometimes recurved. Plumage black and white. Legs long.

Found in most parts of the globe. Breed in north region of N. Africa. Rarely if ever swim. When flying have peculiar Tern-like call. Avocets, from their strongly webbed feet, were classed by Temminck and others near the Flamingo.

Genus **HIMANTOPUS.**

Himantŏpus = a kind of water-bird, in Oppian (circ. A.D. 180); from ἱμάς = a thong, and πούς = a foot.

Bill twice as long as head. Long thin legs.

898. **Himantopus candidus.** THE COMMON STILT.

Candidus = of a glistening white.
Gaj-paon, *India*; **Lalgori, Lamgora,** *Bengal.*

♂ 15½″. Legs lake-red. Bill 2¾″, red, tip black. Back, neck, and tail grey. Wing, back of head black, glossed green. Rest white.

Genus **RECURVIROSTRA.**

Recurvirostra, from *rĕcurvus* = turned back, and *rostrum* = the beak.

Bill turned up, channelled above and below.

899. **Recurvirostra avocetta.** THE COMMON AVOCET.

The Italian name; said to be connected with *avis* = a bird.
Kusya-chaha, *Behar.*

♂ 18″. Legs pale grey. Bill 3½″, black. Crown, nape, lesser coverts, and quills black; the rest white.

Tribe *LATITORES.*

Latito, avi, atum, v. n., to lurk, skulk, &c., to be in the habit of concealing one's self.

Feet very large. Hind toe large. Wings short, often spurred.

Family PALAMEDEIDÆ. SCREAMERS.

Peculiar to America. Feet very large, covered with short skin. Small soft plumes on neck. Of large size. One species (*P. cornuta*) inhabiting marshes on north parts of S. America, and the other (*Chauna*) peculiar to north of S. and C. America.

Family PARRIDÆ.

Feet enormous. Claws strong. Wings spurred.

Subfamily PARRINÆ. JACANAS.

Parra = a bird of ill-omen; supposed to be the Wheatear.

Size moderate. Feet and claws very long and thin.

Jacanas, as called in America, are found in the warmer parts of Asia, Africa, and America. They walk or run easily over the plants that float on the water. Not distantly removed from Ostriches and Cassowaries, they also resemble *Megapodius*. They differ from Rails in their more plump form. The fact of females being much larger than males militates against their association with Plovers. The genus *Parra* is restricted to America.

Genus **METOPIDIUS.**

μετωπίδιος = on the forehead.

With forehead-lappet. Short tail.

900. Metopidius indicus. THE BRONZED-WING JACANA.

Dal-pipi, *Bengal*; **Kattoi**, *Purneah.*

♂ 10″; ♀ 12″. Legs green. Bill yellow.—*In winter*: Face white. Crown chestnut. Front-lappet wanting.—*In summer*: Rich green, with purple reflections. Back and lower tail chestnut.

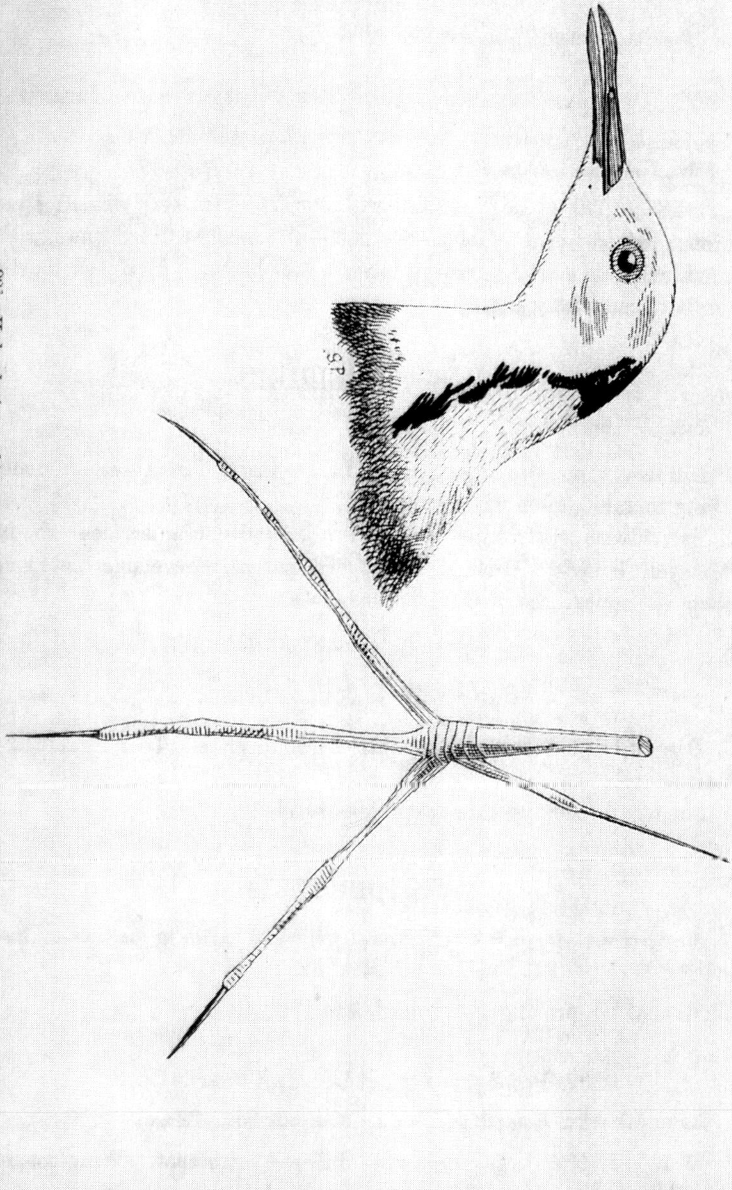

901. *Hydrophasianus chirurgus.* S. Doig, E. Narra, 22-8-75.

Genus **HYDROPHASIANUS.**

ὕδωρ = water; φασιανός = Pheasant.

No forehead-lappet. Tail very long.

901. Hydrophasianus chirurgus. THE PHEASANT-TAILED JACANA.

χειρουργός = a surgeon.
Piho, *India*; **Dalkukra,** *Bengal.*

♂ 18″; ♀ 20″. Legs green. Bill blue, tip green.—*In winter*: Hair brown, barred white. Golden eye-line.—*In summer*: Head white, with black mark on crown. Above olive. Tail black. First and fourth quills tipped with white.

Family RALLIDÆ.

Rallus = thin.

Bill short and wedge-shaped. Large feet. Tail short or none. Wing rounded, often with spur.

Extensively represented in Australia and Oceania; less so in Malayan Islands. General aspect and partially vegetable diet give them the appearance of Gallinaceous birds.

Subfamily GALLINULINÆ.

Base of bill in many expands into a frontal plate. Toes bordered by narrow web.

Scattered generally throughout the world.

Genus **PORPHYRIO.**

Porphyrio = πορφυρίων = a red-coloured water-bird known to the Greeks; from πορφύρα = purple.

Base of bill prolonged to top of head.

902. Porphyrio neglectus. THE PURPLE COOT.

Keim, Kharim, *India*; **Kem,** *Bengal*; **Nila bolakodi** (Telugu).

♂ 18″ to 19″. Legs brick-red. Bill red, with spot. Wing-coverts pale blue. Breast pure blue. Undertail white.

Genus FULICA.

Fulică = a Coot, in classical Latin; akin to φαλ-ακρός = bald-headed.

Shield on forehead. Second and third quills longest.

903. Fulica atra. THE BALD COOT.

Atra = black.
Dasari, *India*; **Bara godhan**, *Purneah*; **Boli kodi** (Telugu).

♂ 15″ to 16″. Legs with three garters. Bill white. Head and neck deep black. Underparts ashy.—*In young*: Underparts grey.

Fulica personata.

♂ 22″. Legs light green. Bill orange. Hind toe has no lobe or web. Tail of 18 feathers, much rounded. Crown bluish grey. Sides drab. Breast, abdomen, lower tail-coverts white. Back and scapulars dark brown.

Genus GALLICREX.

Bill passes over forehead into a horn on top of the head.

904. Gallicrex cristatus. THE COMMON WATER-COCK.

Kora, Khora, *India*.

♂ 16″ to 17″; ♀ 14″. Legs, ♂ dull red; ♀ dull green. Bill red, tip yellow.—*In summer*: Male dull black, edged brown. Edge of wing white.—*Female*: Brown, edged fulvous. Beneath barred brown.

Genus GALLINULA.

Gallinŭla = a chicken; diminutive of *gallina* = a hen.

Small fore shield. Second, third, and fourth quills subequal. Same as "*Gallicrex*;" but smaller.

905. Gallinula chloropus. THE COMMON WATER-HEN.

Chlŏrŏpus = green-footed, from χλωρός + πούς.
Godhan, *Behar*; **Jumbu Kodi** (Telugu); **Jal murghi**, *Bengal*.

♂ 13″; ♀ 12″. Legs with orange garter. Bill red, tip yellow. Head grey. Above olive. Beneath grey. Flanks streaked white. Undertail white.

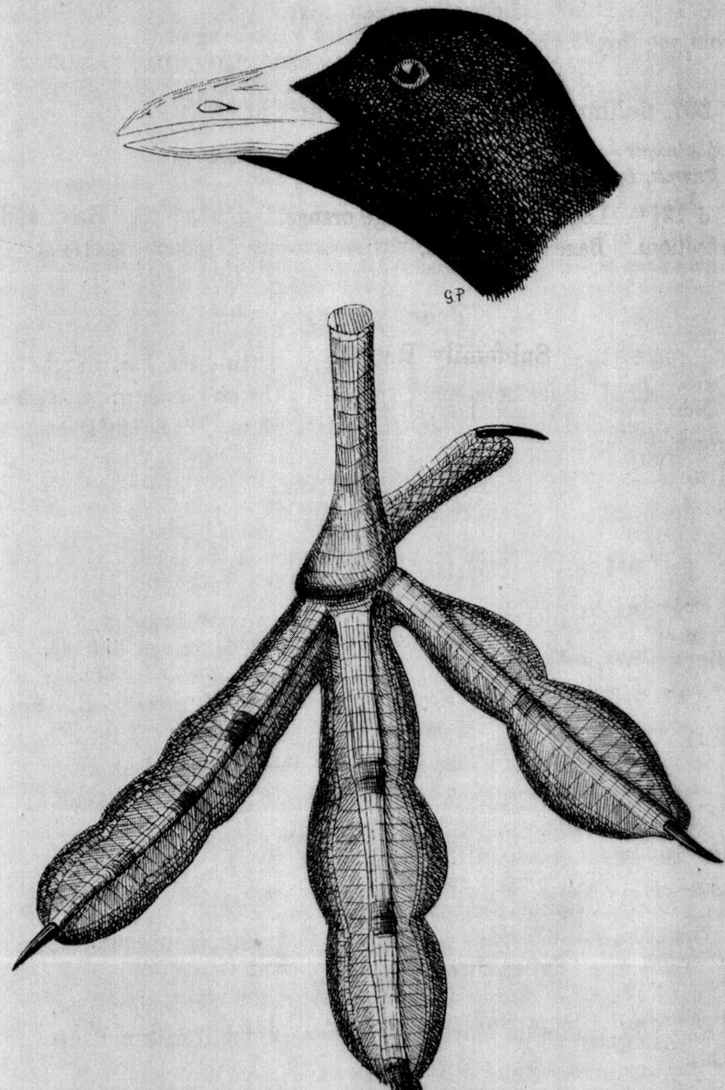

903. *Fulica atra.* 22-10-75.

Gallinula burnesi. THE SMALL WATER-HEN.

Gajra, *Sind.*

♂ 11½″; ♀ 11″. Legs olive-green. Front-plate small or wanting. Chin and throat white.

907. Gallinula phœnicura. THE WHITE-BREASTED WATER-HEN.

φοινίκουρος = a bird.
Dawak, *India*; **Kureyn**, *Gondwarra*; **Kurayi**, *Sind.*

♂ 12¾″. Legs green. Bill ridge orange. Above black, with green reflections. Beneath chestnut.

Subfamily RALLINÆ. RAILS.

No frontal plate. Beak much compressed. Plumage soft and loose, brown, streaked, and often banded. Sexes alike in colour. Mostly of small size. Found in most parts. Many true Rails in America. The Corn-Crake (*Crex pratensis*) is common in Afghanistan.

Genus PORZANA.

Porzāna, the Italian name; also written *Sforzana* (Salvadori) and *Forzane.* Of unknown derivation.

Bill equals length of head, somewhat narrowed in middle. Wings rounded. Tail short. Toes long, slender, and smooth. Sharp claws.

908. Porzana akool. THE BROWN RAIL.

♂ 10½″ to 12″; 4 to 6 oz. ♀ 10″ to 11½″; 3½ to 5 oz. Legs dull lake-red. Bill green.—*Male*: Head black. Above olive-brown. Wings and tail dusky. Undertail deep brown. White chin.

909. Porzana maruetta. THE SPOTTED RAIL.

Maruetta, Latinized from the French *la Marouette.* The word is probably not Italian, as it is not mentioned by Salvadori.
Khairi, *Bengal*; **Venna-mudi-kodi** (Telugu).

♂ 8½″ to 9″; 3 to 4 oz. Legs bright green. Bill orange and yellow. Above olive-brown, blotched. All feathers spotted and streaked white. Nape black and white.

Porzana parva. THE LITTLE RAIL.

♂ 8″; 1¾ oz. ♀ 7¾″ to 8″; 1¼ to 1½ oz. Legs yellow-green. Bill yellow-green, red base. Throat and breast ashy, banded white on abdomen. Above dark brown, splotched black.

910. Porzana pygmæa. THE PIGMY OR BAILLON'S RAIL.

BAILLONI, in honour of Louis Antoine François Baillon, of Abbeville, who died about 1855. He first found the species in Picardy, and gave Vieillot details of its habits &c.

♂ 6½″ to 7¾″; 1 to 2 oz. Legs yellow-green. Bill ⅔″, dark green. Above yellow-brown, with white irregular spots black-edged. Beneath grey. Undertail black, with white cross-bar.

911. Porzana fusca. THE RUDDY RAIL.

♂ 7⅔″ to 8¾″. Legs red. Bill red, tip green. Above olive-brown. Vent and undertail barred white. Head and breast deep red.

Porzana bicolor. ELWES'S RAIL.

♂ 8″ to 9″. Legs brown. Bill greenish. Head, neck, and breast ashy. Back and wings chestnut. (H. & M. ii. 217.)

Porzana cinerea. THE WHITY-BROWN RAIL.

♂ 8½″; 2¼ oz. Legs green. Bill brown-red. Above dark brown, mottled. Below white. Black eye-streak.

Porzana fasciata. THE MALAYAN BANDED RAIL.

♂ 8⅓″ to 9¾″; 2¾ to 4¾ oz. Legs coral-red. Bill slaty. Orbital ring, gape, and skin of chin vermilion. Chin and throat whitish. Sides of neck and breast chestnut. Above chestnut. Abdomen heavily banded black and white. (H. & M. ii. 235.)

912. Porzana ceylonica. THE BANDED RAIL.

♂ 9¾″ to 10¾″. Legs pale green. Bill 1⅓″, green. Same as *P. fusca*, but larger.—*Male*: Crown, nape, and back of neck rich chestnut; but *in female* same colour as the back.

Genus RALLUS.

Rallus, the Latinized form of the French *Râle* (spelt *Rasle* in Bélon, 1555); our *Rail*, Dutch *Ral*; akin to *rattle*.

Bill longer, tip slightly curved and grooved for ⅔ of length. Forehead spiny.

Rallus canningi. The Andamanese Banded Crake.

Crex = κρέξ, a Rail, in classical Greek. Cf. κρέκω = I strike so as to sound.

♂ 13″ to 14½″. Legs olive-green. Bill 1⅓″, pale green. Head, neck, and above chestnut. Below black, banded white. (H. & M. ii. 241.)

913. Rallus striatus. The Blue-breasted Rail.

Wade-kodi (Telugu).

♂ 9⅔″ to 11½″; 3½ to 5 oz. Legs dingy pink. Bill 1½″, reddish. Above olive, with narrow white bars edged black. Vent and under-tail dull, with white bands. Face, neck, and breast blue-grey. White banding on wings.

Rallus obscurior. The Andamanese Banded Rail.

♂ 11½″ to 12¾″. Legs slaty green. Bill 1¾″. Indian-red. Face, sides of neck, and breast lead-grey. Forehead and crown dark maroon. Above dark brown, banded white. (H. & M. ii. 253.)

914. Rallus indicus. The Indian Rail.

♂ 10½″ to 12″; 4½ to 6 oz. Legs dingy pink. Bill 1½″, dull red. Above olive-brown, with black streaks. Streak below eye. Under-tail white, rufous, and black.

Rallus aquaticus. The Water-Rail.

Aquăticus = living in or by the water, *ăqua*.

♂ 12″; 3 to 5 oz. Legs flesh-brown. Bill 1⅔″, red. More grey than *R. indicus*. No facial stripe. (H. & M. ii. 261.)

(B) *Young helpless at birth.*

Tribe *CULTIROSTRES.*

Culter = a knife; *rostrum* = a bill.

Bill thick, pointed or slightly curved. Wings ample. Hind toe on same plane as anterior.

STORKS have bill very stout and thick, and are of large size.

HERONS have bill more slender and pointed, with middle toe more or less serrated.

IBISES have bill more or less curved.

Family CICONIIDÆ. STORKS.

Bill large, long, and straight. All anterior toes joined at base. Of large size.

Inhabit India and its Archipelago, Africa, and America. Flight powerful. A few migratory and gregarious. Breed in lofty trees. Giants of the Bird Kingdom.

Genus **LEPTOPTILOS.**

λεπτός = thin; πτίλον = a wing.

Bill enormous. Head more or less nude. Undertail somewhat decomposed, and called Marabou feathers.

915. Leptoptilos argala. THE GIGANTIC OR ADJUTANT STORK.

Hargila, Dusta, *India*; **Chaniari-dank,** *Bengal*; **Garur,** *N. W. P.*; **Pini-gala-konga** (Telugu).

♂ 60″. ♀ 55″. Legs grey-white. Bill 12″, greenish. Head bare, with long neck-pouch. Wing-band silver-grey, very conspicuous. Above slaty, glossed green.—*In winter*: No wing-band and pouch yellowish.

916. Leptoptilos javanica. THE HAIR-CRESTED OR SMALL ADJUTANT STORK.

Madan-chur, *Bengal*; **Chinjura,** *India*; **Bang-gor,** *Purneah*; **Dodal-konga** (Telugu).

♂ 54″. Legs dirty black. Bill 10″, dirty. Bald, bare neck. Thin mane. White neck-ruff. Above gloss-green, faintly barred.

Genus MYCTERIA.

μυκτηρίζω = to turn up the nose.

Bill large, solid. Tip ascending.

917. Mycteria australis. THE BLACK-NECKED STORK.

♂ 52″ to 56″. Legs red. Bill black. Under plumage white, rest glossy green.

Genus CICONIA.

Cĭcōnia = a Stork, in classical Latin. Cognate with *căno* = I sing, κύκνος = a Swan, καναχή = a sharp sound, κόναβος = a din.

Bill convex above; tip below inclining upwards. Toes strongly webbed. Third and fourth quills longest.

918. Ciconia nigra. THE BLACK STORK.

Surmai, *India*.

♂ 44″; 9 lbs. ♀ 39½″; 7½ lbs. Legs dark red. Bill blood-red. Breast and abdomen white; rest blackish, with purple reflections.

919. Ciconia alba. THE WHITE STORK.

Laglag, *India*; **Dhak**, *N. W. P.*; **Wadume konga** (Telugu).

♂ 42″. Legs red. Bill blood-red. Greater coverts and quills black, rest white.

920. Ciconia leucocephala. THE WHITE-NECKED STORK.

Manikjor, Kali, Laglag, *India*; **Kandesur** (Mahratta); **Sanku-budi-konga** (Telugu).

♂ 36″ to 37″. Legs dull red. Bill dusky. Neck and tail white; rest black-glossed. Face and ear-patch nude.

Family ARDEIDÆ. HERONS.

Bill very sharp and deeply cleft. Outer toe only joined to middle one. Middle toe more or less serrated.

Subfamily PSOPHINÆ. TRUMPETERS.

Inhabit Tropical South America. Two genera, *Psophia* and *Cariama*.

Subfamily Ardeinæ.

Genus **ARDEA.**

Ardĕa = a Heron, in Virgil, Georg. i. 364. Cognate with the classical Greek ἐρωδιός, of which the supposed primitive form, ῥωδιός, occurs in Hipponax (about 546 B.C.). Old Norse *arta* = a Teal.

Bill with groove from nostrils towards tip. Outer toe joined to middle one by web. Second, third, and fourth quills subequal and longest.

921. Ardea goliat. The Giant Heron.

Darya anjan, *Bengal.*

♂ 60″. Legs black. Bill dusky, tip green. Stands nearly 4 feet. Upper plumage grey. Short brown crest. Below chestnut-brown.—*Young* have dense crest.

922. Ardea fusca. The Dusky Heron.

Anjan, *Bengal*; **San barado,** *Sind.*

♂ 46″. Legs green-grey. Bill yellow. Narrow crest as long as 8″. Breast-plumes and long scapulars silver-grey.

Ardea sumatrana.

♂ 50″. Legs dirty green. Bill yellowish. A sea-coast bird. Breast, abdomen, lower tail-coverts, wing-lining, axillaries, and lower back dirty ash. Broad bare space above and below the eye dirty green. Above slaty. (S. F. vi. 469.)

923. Ardea cinerea. The Common Heron.

Cinerea = ash-coloured, from *cinis* = ashes.

Kabud, *India*; **Anjan, Sada-kanka,** *Bengal*; **Saa,** *Sind*; **Khyra,** *Behar*; **Narraina pachi** (Telugu); **Narrayan** (Tamil).

♂ 39″. Legs brown. Bill dark yellow. Narrow crest of black. Neck white. Long grey scapulars. Neck-feathers spotted black, form pectoral plume.

924. Ardea purpurea. The Purple Heron.

Nari, *India*; **Lalkank,** *Bengal*; **Pamula nari-gadu** (Telugu).

♂ 36″ to 42″. Legs red-brown. Bill deep yellow. Three narrow black cheek-bands. Scapulars purple, forming plume.

Genus **HERODIAS.**

ἐρωδιός = a Crane.

Bill slender and straight. Neck long. Tibia naked for half its length. Plumage white.

Herodias alba. THE GREAT WHITE HERON OR EGRET.

Bill 5″, yellow in winter, black in summer.—*In summer*: No crest. No pectoral plumes. Dorsal train long, of decomposed feathers extending 5″ beyond tail. (S. F. vi. 480.)

925. Herodias torra. THE INDIAN LARGE WHITE HERON.

♂ 36″. Legs black. Bill $3\frac{3}{4}''$ to $4\frac{1}{2}''$; yellow in winter, black in summer.—*In summer*: No crest, no pectoral plumes. Dorsal train extends about 4″ beyond tail. Orbital skin pea-green.

926. Herodias intermedia. THE SMALLER WHITE HERON OR EGRET.

Patokha bagla, *India.*

♂ 27″ to 28″. Legs black. Bill $2\frac{2}{3}''$ to 3″; yellow in winter, black in summer.—*In summer*: No crest. Pectoral plume of long decomposed feathers. Dorsal train extending about 7″ beyond tail.

927. Herodias garzetta. THE LITTLE WHITE HERON OR EGRET.

Kilchia, *India*; **Nella muka konga** (Telugu).

♂ 24″ to 25″. Legs black. Bill 3″ to $3\frac{1}{2}''$, black.—*In summer*: Crest on head of two or three feathers 5″ to 6″ long. Dorsal train curving up, scarcely extending beyond tail. Pectoral plume of narrow ordinary feathers.

Herodias eulophotes.

♂ 27″. Legs green-black. Bill $3\frac{1}{2}''$ to 4″, black.—*In summer*: Crest full of numerous narrow feathers, the longest $4\frac{1}{2}''$. Dorsal train and pectoral plume of narrow ordinary feathers. (S. F. vi. 480.)

Genus **DEMIEGRETTA.**

Adult dark. Young birds white.

928. Demiegretta gularis. THE ASHY EGRET.

♂ 24″ to $27\frac{1}{2}''$. Legs black. Bill red-yellow. Crest on head. Short dorsal train. Breast plumes narrow and pointed.—*In winter*: Throat only white.

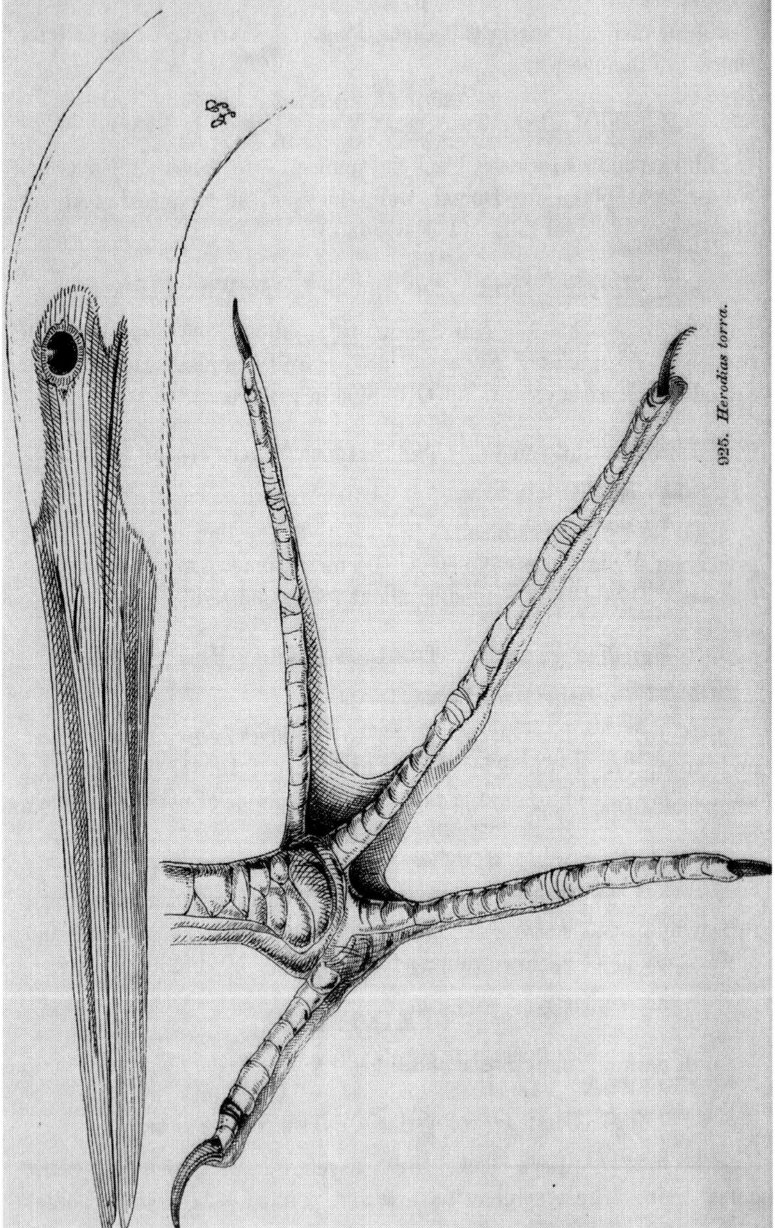

925. *Herodias torra.*

Demiegretta sacra.

♂ 21″ to 24″. Legs green. Bill yellowish.—*In summer*: Above slate. Head almost black. Pectoral and dorsal plumes slate-grey. Crest about 1″. (S. F. ii. 305.)

Genus BUPHUS.

Bill stout and curved at tip.

929. Buphus coromandus. THE CATTLE EGRET.

Doria bagla, Gai bagla, *Bengal*; **Samti konga** (Telugu).

♂ 21″. Legs greenish. Bill yellow in winter, orange in summer. Head, crest, breast, and dorsal plumes golden buff.—*In winter*: Plumage white.

Genus ARDEOLA.

Ardeŏla, diminutive of *Ardĕa*. *Ardĕa*, *æ*, f. = ἐρωδιός = a Heron (Virgil, Georg. i. 364).

Tibia feathered to the knee nearly.

930. Ardeola grayi. THE PADDY-BIRD OR POND-HERON.

♂ $18\frac{1}{2}$″. Legs dull green. Bill blue, yellow, and black. Crest white. Neck yellow. Back maroon.—*In winter*: Head, breast, and thigh fulvous.

Ardeola prasinosceles.

♂ 21″; 11 oz. Legs bright orange. Bill black, yellow, and pale blue. Chin and neck-stripe white. Head and back of neck chestnut. Crest of long pointed feathers; longest 4″. Breast and side-feathers disintegrated. Back black; rest of bird white. (S. F. ii. 481.)

Genus BUTORIDES.

Inner toe short. Neck thick and short.

931. Butorides javanica. THE GREEN HERON.

♂ 16″ to 17″. Legs greenish. Bill black and yellow. Head black. Back green. Central line to breast white.

Genus **ARDETTA.**

Ardetta, diminutive of *Ardea* = a Heron, on the analogy of the Italian *Garzetta* &c. In Pliny the diminutive is *Ardeŏla.*

Toes long, and claws strong. Of small size. Of nocturnal habits. These may be said to be BITTERNS with EGRET bills.

932. **Ardetta flavicollis.** THE BLACK BITTERN.

♂ 23″ to 24″. Legs pale brown. Bill red-brown.—*In summer*: Golden stripe on sides of neck. Neck-feathers mixed white, brown, and black.

Ardetta cinnamomea. THE CHESTNUT BITTERN.

♂ 16″. Legs greenish. Bill yellow. Pectoral gorget dark brown in centre.—*Young birds*: Feathers brown, with yellow edges.

934. **Ardetta sinensis.** THE YELLOW BITTERN.

♂ 14″ to 15″. ♀ 6 oz. Legs pale green. Bill pale yellow. Top of head, quills, and tail black.

935. **Ardetta minuta.** THE LITTLE BITTERN.

Mĭnūta = small, from *mĭnŭo* = I diminish.

♂ 14″. Legs greenish. Bill yellow. Head, back, and tail black.

Genus **BOTAURUS.**

Botaurus = a Bittern, in late Latin; probably akin to our "Bittern." French *butor*, &c. Certainly not derived from *bos*+*taurus*, though perhaps confused therewith in popular etymology.

Long lax feathers. Plumage game. Toe longer than tarsus.

936. **Botaurus stellaris.** THE COMMON BITTERN.

♂ 26″ to 30″. Legs greenish. Bill yellow and brown. Moustache black. Neck yellow, with brown spots.

Genus **GOISAKIUS.**

Short thick neck. Middle toe shorter than the tarsus.

Goisakius melanolophus.

♀ 17″ to 19″; ¾ lb. Mantle dull chestnut, finely barred black-brown.

Rump and upper tail-coverts slate. First three primaries blackish, broadly tipped white; others tipped chestnut. Wing-lining, axillaries, flanks, and under tail-coverts barred black and white. (S. F. ii. 512.)

Genus **NYCTICORAX.**

νυκτικόραξ = a Nightjar in Aristotle, a Screech-Owl in the Anthology (xi. 186); but strictly a "Night-Raven," from *νύξ*+*κόραξ*.

Third quill longest. Tarsus scaled.

937. Nycticorax griseus. THE COMMON NIGHT-HERON.

♂ 21″ to 24″. Legs greenish. Bill black. Eye-streak white. Back black, glossed green. Crest of narrow feathers fitting into each other.

The Boat-bill of South America (*Cancroma cochlearia*) is evidently a Heron; the Whale-bill of Africa (*Balæniceps rex*) is another nearly related form, and the Umbre (*Scopus umbretta*) is usually considered as belonging to this family.

Family TANTALIDÆ.

Bill hard, long, cylindrical, and curved. Front toes joined at base by web.

The Ibises and Spoonbills are said not to belong to the same group as Herons. They inhabit warmer parts of Asia, Africa, and America. They hunt about for their food.

Subfamily TANTALINÆ.

Bill very large, thick, rounded, and smooth.

Genus **TANTALUS.**

Tantălus, King of Phrygia, ancestor of the Pelopidæ (akin to *τάλαντον*, *ταλάνταω*, *ταντάλοω*), probably in relation to the mythological story of his *hanging balanced* over water.

Tip of bill bent down, emarginated.

938. Tantalus leucocephalus. THE PELICAN IBIS.

♂ 42″. Legs fleshy. Bill deep yellow. Plumage white. Tertiaries rosy, with darker band and tipped white.

Subfamily PLATALEINÆ.

Bill broad, flat, and depressed.

Genus PLATALEA.

Plătălĕa = the Spoonbill, in Cicero, N. D. ii. 49, 124. *Plătĕa*, in Pliny, H. N. x. 40, 56, probably from πλατύς = broad.

Bill like a spatula. Second quill longest.

939. Platalea leucorodia. THE SPOONBILL IBIS.

Leucŏrŏdia = the late Latin form of λευκερωδιός; from λευκός = white, ἐρωδιός = a Heron.

♂ 31″ to 36″. Legs black. Bill black, tip yellow. Breast-patch buff-yellow, extending towards back. Crest long.—*Female* smaller.

Subfamily ANASTOMATINÆ.

Bill thick, coarse, and gaping in the middle.

Genus ANASTOMUS.

Ἀνα = up and down; στόμα = a mouth.

Second and third quills subequal.

940. Anastomus oscitans. THE SHELL IBIS.

♂ 29″ to 32″. Legs fleshy. Bill green. Plumage ash-grey. Wing and tail black. Some nearly white, supposed to be adults.

Subfamily IBISINÆ.

Ἶβις = the Ibis, an Egyptian bird to which divine honours were paid.

Bill long, thin, curved, and channelled. Breed on trees.

Genus THRESKIORNIS.

Head and neck nude and black.

941. Threskiornis melanocephalus. THE WHITE IBIS.

♂ 29″. Legs black. Bill black. Plumage white, glossed green. Tertiaries with open barbs.

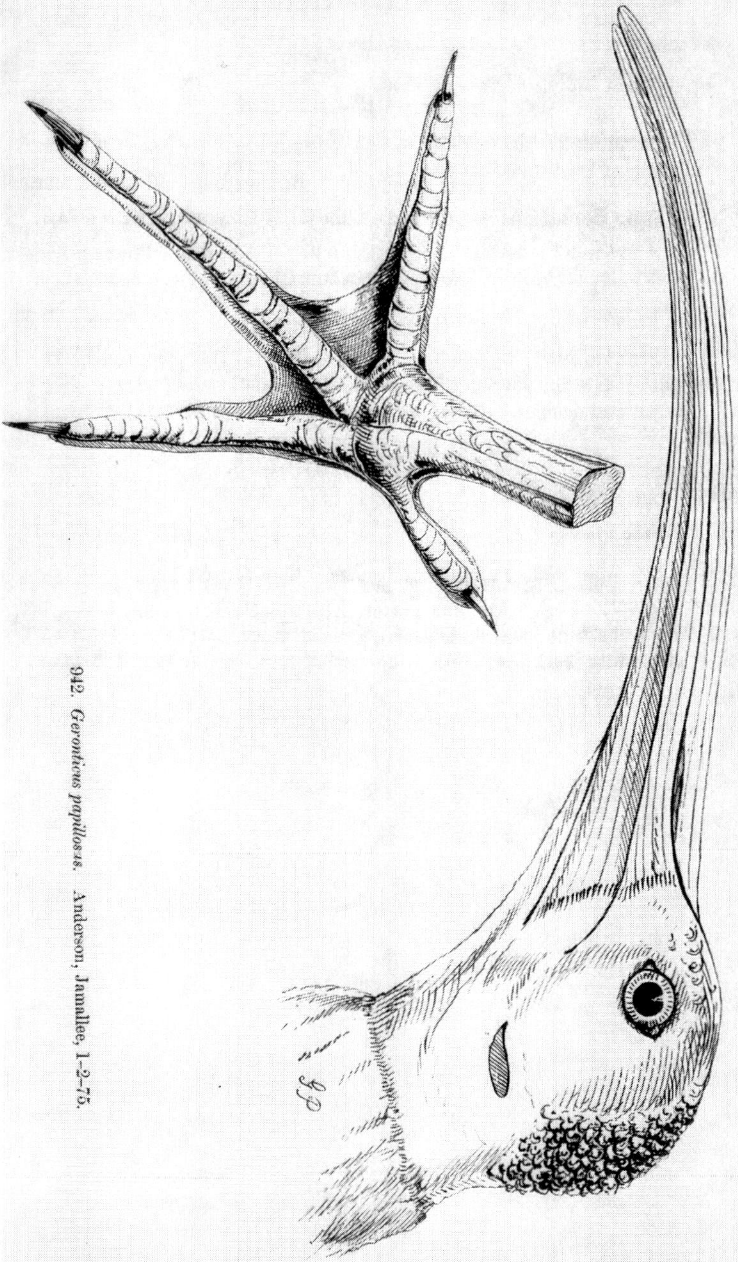

942. *Geronticus papillosus.* Anderson, Jamallee, 1-2-75.

Genus GERONTICUS.

γεροντικός = old age, or belonging to an old man.

Top of head nude. Tarsus scaled.

942. Geronticus papillosus. The King Curlew or Black Ibis.

♂ 25″ to 30″; 3¼ lbs. Legs brick-red. Bill leaden. Plumage black. Red warts on back of head. Wings and tail steel-blue. Sexes alike.

Geronticus davisoni.

♂ 32″ to 32½″; 3½ to 4 lbs. Legs coral-red. Bill plumbeous. Head black; anterior portion only covered with small brown warts; none on crown and occiput. Broad white necklet. (S. F. iii. 300.)

Genus FALCINELLUS.

Falx, falcis, f. = a sickle.

Face nude.

943. Falcinellus igneus. The Glossy Ibis.

♂ 22″. Legs with blue garter. Bill blackish. Head, breast, and below chestnut; rest dark green, glossed purple.—*Young*: Ash-brown, with white markings.

NATATORES.

WATER BIRDS.

NATATORES. (SWIMMERS.)

WATER BIRDS.

Order.	Sub-order.	Tribe.		Fa[mily]
Legs placed far back. Plumage thick and close, with quantity of down. Hind toe small or wanting. FEET MORE OR LESS FULLY WEBBED.	Young following the parent as soon as hatched.	*LAMELLIROSTRES.* — Broad bill, covered with soft skin and edged with thin lamellæ; the tip alone horny	Food chiefly vegetable.	**PHŒNICOPTERIDÆ.** Bill suddenly bent dow
				CYGNIDÆ.—Lengthen high at base and of e very large size. Sexes
				ANSERIDÆ.—Bill sho hind. Plumage of sex
				ANATIDÆ.—Bill broa width or wider at tip, differ greatly ....
				MERGIDÆ.—Bill cyli well bent over. Head
		MERGITORES. — Bill long, straight, and pointed. Hind toe lobed	Food chiefly fishes, crustacea, or insects.	**COLYMBIDÆ.**—Short Anterior toes complet preference to fresh wat
				PODICIPIDÆ.—Toes web. Tail almost w Head often tufted. Y
		VAGATORES.—Bill hooked at tip or pointed. Wings long and pointed		**PROCELLARIDÆ.**— as if joined. Nostrils
				LARIDÆ. — Nostrils generally present. Pl and brown ....
	Young requiring to be fed for a time.	*PISCATORES.* — Feet entirely webbed, and hind toe joined to inner front toe by web. Legs short		**PHAËTONIDÆ.** — C Bill finely dentated .
				SULIDÆ.—Bill stout.
				ATTAGENIDÆ. — Bi downwards ....
				PELECANIDÆ.—Hu
				GRACULIDÆ.—Bill Tail stiff. Plumage l
		URINATORES.—Usually three toes only, or with small hind toe pointing forwards		**ALCIDÆ.**—Bill high toe. Three anterior t Fly badly. Swim an
				SPHENISCIDÆ.—W kind of fin, with scal on the sea ....

* Not re[p]

...y.	Subfamily.	Genus.	Page
...Neck and leg of great length.	....	FLAMINGOES	101
...neck. Short legs. Bill ...l breadth throughout. Of ...e; no seasonal change ..	....	SWANS	103
	ANSERINÆ............	TRUE GEESE	104
	CEREOPSINÆ	NEW-HOLLAND GEESE*	107
...narrower in front than be-	PLECTROPTERINÆ ..	SPUR GEESE	107
...iffers slightly............	NETTOPODINÆ........	COTTON TEAL	108
	TADORNINÆ	WHISTLING TEAL	108
		SHELLDRAKES................	109
...at base than high, of equal ...h numerous lamellæ. Sexes	ANATINÆ	TRUE DUCKS (RIVER)	110
		TEAL.......................	118
....	FULIGULINÆ	POCHARDS (SEA) OR DIVING DUCKS	121
...cal, edged with teeth; tip ...re or less crested	....	MERGANSERS	124
...il, and can stand upright. ...webbed. Frequent seas in	....	IMBERS, DIVERS, OR LOONS*....	125
..., bordered with large loose ...ng. Under-plumage silky. ...g striped black and white..	....	GREBES	126
	DIOMEDINÆ	ALBATROSSES*	127
...much hooked, and appears	PROCELLARINÆ......	PETRELS	128
...tained in one tube........	PUFFININÆ	PUFFIN PETRELS	129
	HALODROMINÆ	DIVING PETRELS..............	130
	LESTRIDINÆ	SKUAS	130
...ear and basal. Hind toe	LARINÆ	GULLS	131
...age grey and white, or black	STERNINÆ	TERNS	136
		NODDIES	143
		SCISSOR-BILLS	143
...al tail-feathers very long.	.... (These might all be included under one family:—PELECANIDÆ.)	TROPIC-BIRDS	144
...ail wedge-shaped	....	BOOBIES	145
...ong; both mandibles bent		FRIGATE-BIRDS	145
...bill, with pouch		PELICANS	146
...indric, hooked, and grooved. ...k	....	CORMORANTS	147
		DARTERS	149
...sharp on culmen. No hind ...fully webbed. Short wings. ...ive well..................	ALCINÆ	AUKS*	149
		PUFFINS*	149
	URIINÆ	GUILLEMOTS*	149
...s reduced in some cases to a ...athers. Live almost entirely	....	PENGUINS*	149

...ented in India.

Order **NATATORES.** *WATER BIRDS.*

Swimmers.

So variously organized that few generalizations can be made. The connections of this order are not very apparent. Some imagine that it is related on one side through the Geese with the *Rasores*, others through the Grebes with the Coots. Again, the Frigate-birds show a decided tendency towards *Raptores*.

FEET MORE OR LESS FULLY WEBBED. Legs placed far back. Plumage thick, close, with quantity of down. Hind toe small or wanting.

(A) *The young following the parent as soon as hatched.*

Tribe *LAMELLIROSTRES.*

Lamella = a small plate; *rostrum* = a bill.

Food chiefly vegetable. Broad bill, covered with soft skin and edged with thin lamellæ. The tip alone horny.

Family PHŒNICOPTERIDÆ.

Neck and leg of great length. Bill suddenly bent down. Have fleshy tongue and anatomical structure of Ducks. Found in warmer parts of the world.

Genus **PHŒNICOPTERUS.**

φοινικόπτερος = red-feathered.

Bill high at base and suddenly bent down. First and second quills subequal and longest. Fifth remix present in wing.

944. Phœnicopterus antiquus. THE COMMON FLAMINGO.

Bag-hans, Raj-hans, *India*; **Pukonga** (Telugu); **Pu-nari** (Tamil).

♂ 52″; 10 lbs. ♀ 42″. Legs rose-red. Bill rosy, black tip. Plumage rosy white. Quills black.—*Young* mixed brown and dusky.

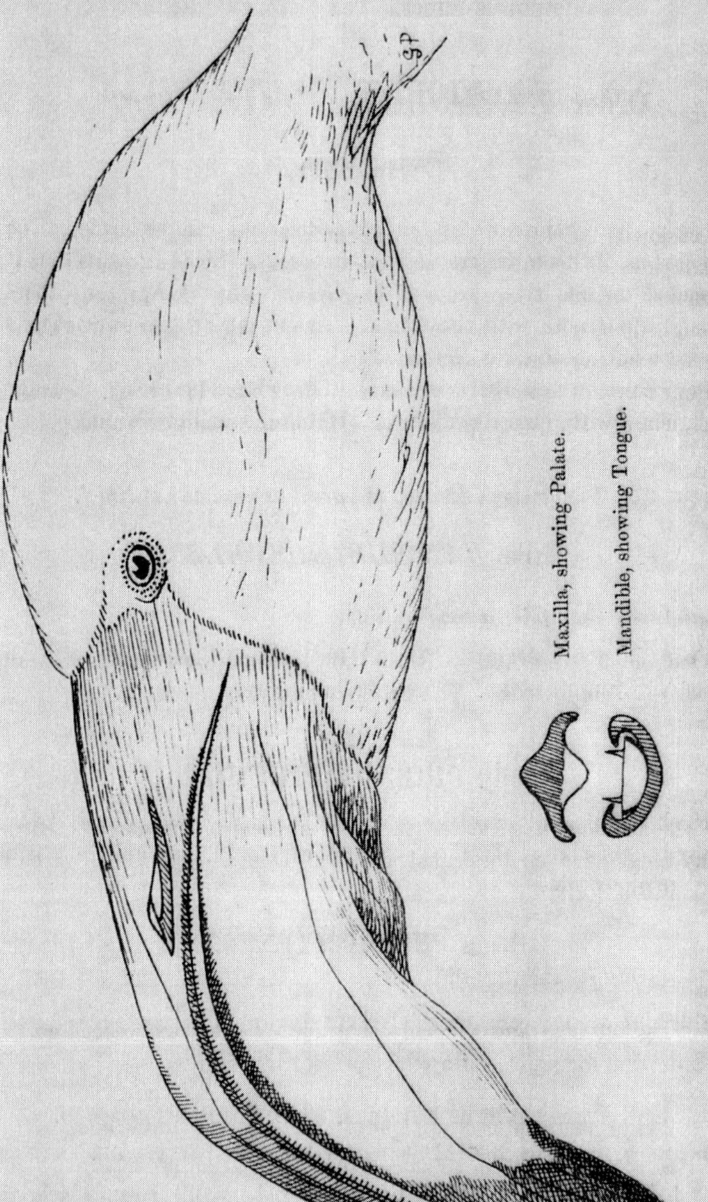

944. *Phœnicopterus antiquus.* Kurrachee, 6–3–61.

Phœnicopterus minor. THE SMALLER FLAMINGO.

♂ 33″ to 34″. ♀ 30″. Legs deep red. Bill red, tip black.—*In winter*: Pale rosy.—*In summer*: Bright rose, with cherry-coloured plumes on scapulars. (S. F. i. 35.)

Family CYGNIDÆ.

Lengthened neck, but short legs. Bill high at base and of equal breadth throughout. Of very large size. Feed on seeds, roots of water-plants, and also on grass. Sexes alike, no seasonal change.

Genus **CYGNUS.**

κύκνος = a Swan.

Bill covered with short fleshy core that extends in a point to the eye on each side. Nostrils more or less in middle of bill, rather oblique and oval. Second and third quills equal and longest. Hind toe short and without any marginal lobe.

Cygnus olor. THE MUTE SWAN.
(The "Tame Swan" of Europe.)

Ŏlor = a Swan, in classical Latin, especially in poetry. Perhaps a Spanish word. *Cf.* Welsh *alarch.*
Penr, *Punjab*; **Koday**, *Yarkand.*

♂ 55½″; 15 lbs. ♀ 53″; 13 lbs. Legs black. Bill red-orange. Plumage white, with cream or buff tinge. Tail comparatively long and wedge-shaped. (H. & M. iii. 41.)

Cygnus musicus. THE HOOPER SWAN.

Mūsicus = musical; from *Mūsa* = the Muse.

♂ 60″; 19 lbs. ♀ 52″; 16½ lbs. Legs black. Bill black. No protuberance on bill. Basal part of bill bright yellow. Frontal feathers prolonged into an angle. Plumage white. (H. & M. iii. 47.)

Cygnus bewicki. BEWICK'S SWAN.

Bewicki, named after Thomas Bewick (b. 1753, d. 1828), author of the 'History of British Birds.'

♂ 42″ to 50″. ♀ 39″ to 40″. Legs black. Bill black. No protuberance on bill. Bare space from eye to nostril yellow. Plumage white and light grey-brown.—*Young birds* brown.

Family ANSERIDÆ.

Bill short, narrower in front than behind. Plumage of sexes differs slightly. Live in flocks, breeding mostly in Polar regions.

Subfamily ANSERINÆ. TRUE GEESE.

Bill short, high at base, and conical. Laminar teeth more or less exposed. Large heavy body, with long neck and small head.

Genus **ANSER.**

Anser, anseris = a Goose.

Bill at base as high as head. Of large size and grey plumage. Bill pale. Legs usually reddish.

945. Anser cinereus. THE LAG OR GREY GOOSE.

Cĭnĕrĕus = ash-coloured; from *cĭnĕres* = ashes.
Raj-hans, Hans, *India*; **Kallank, Karhans,** *Bhaugulpore*; **Sona,** *N. W. P.*; **Mogala,** *Nepal*; **Kangnai,** *Manipar*; **Ghaz,** *Kashgar.*

♀ 30″ to 35″; 5¾ to 9 lbs. Legs tile-red. Bill fleshy, tip white. Head and neck dove-brown, tinged grey. Irides deep brown.

Anser segetum. THE BEAN-GOOSE.

Sĕgĕtum = gen. pl. of *sĕges* = a cornfield.

♀ 31″. Legs orange-yellow. Bill black, with orange band. Like the Grey-lag, but smaller. Colour nearly uniform. (H. & M. iii. 67.)

946. Anser brachyrhynchus. THE PINK-FOOTED GOOSE.

Short-beaked, from βραχύς + ῥύγχος.

♀ 26″ to 30″; 6 lbs. ♀ 5 lbs. Legs pink. Bill red, nail black. Head and neck brown. Body brown, with white waves. First and second primaries bluish, others black.

947. Anser albifrons. THE WHITE-FRONTED OR LAUGHING GOOSE.

Albĭfrons = with a white forehead; from *albus* + *frons.*

♂ 26″ to 28″; 4½ to 5½ lbs. Legs orange. Bill purple, nail white. Forehead and cheeks white, with brown band. Above ash-brown. Beneath white, with black cross bands.

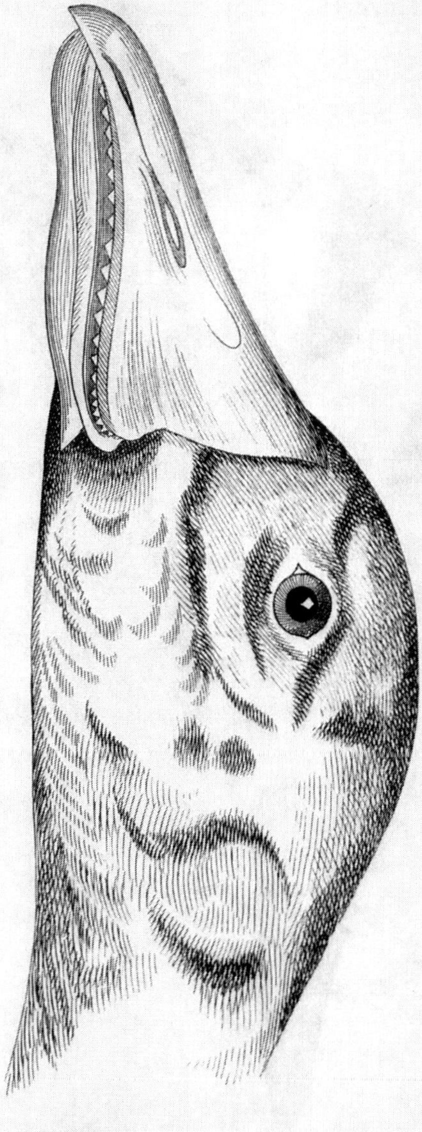

945. *Anser cinereus.*

949. *Anser indicus.* Rookun, 9–12–74.

948. **Anser minutus.** THE DWARF GOOSE.

♂ 22″; 4 lbs. Legs red. Bill orange. Back and scapulars dark grey, with cross bands. Primaries grey. Abdomen black, bordered white. Flanks dark grey.

949. **Anser indicus.** THE BARRED-HEADED GOOSE.

Indicus = Indian; from its native country.

Birooa, Raj-hans, *N. W. P.*; **Paria,** *Nepal*; **Nang-pa,** *Ladak*; **Dod-sarle-hake,** *Mysore*; **Neer bathoo,** *Coimbatore*; **Kangnai,** *Manipur*; **Badi-hans,** *Chittagong.*

♂ 27¼″ to 33½″; 4 to 7 lbs. Legs orange. Bill yellow. Two bars on head and neck. Above ash-grey. Flanks cinnamon.

Subfamily CEREOPSINÆ. NEW-HOLLAND GEESE.

Peculiar to Australia. Seldom enter water. Appear to have affinities both with *Rasores* and *Grallatores.*

Subfamily PLECTROPTERINÆ.

Wing with one spur or more.

Genus **SARCIDIORNIS.**

σαρκίδιον; from *σάρξ* = a bit of flesh, and *ὄρνις* = a bird.

Bill with fleshy boss. Plumage black and white.

950. **Sarcidiornis melanonotus.** THE COMB DUCK OR BLACK-BACKED SPUR GOOSE.

Nukhta, *India*; **Nukwa,** *Chota Nagpur*; **Jutu chillawa** (Telugu); **Neer-koli,** *Coimbatore*; **Tanbay,** *Pegu*; **Bowkban** (Karen).

♂ 30″ to 34″; 6 lbs. ♀ 26″. Legs greenish. Bill black. Head and neck white, spotted. Above black, glossed purple. Back ash-grey.—*Female*: No boss on bill.

Subfamily NETTOPODINÆ.

Bill small, high at base.

Genus **NETTOPUS.**

νῆττα = a Duck; from *νέω* = I swim, and *ποῦς* = a foot.

Bill narrowing in front. Lamellæ concealed. Tail rounded, of 12 feathers.

951. **Nettopus coromandelicus.** The Cotton Teal or White-bodied Goose Teal.

Girri, *India*; **Gur-gurrah,** *Etawah*; **Bullia-hans,** *Dacca*; **Ade adla,** *Rutnagiri*; **Chik-sarle-haki,** *Mysore*; **Neer-akee,** *Coimbatore*; **Karagat,** *Arakan.*

♂ 12½″ to 14″; 8 to 11 oz. ♀ 12½″ to 12¾″; 6½ to 9 oz. Legs greenish. Bill black. Face, neck, and below white. Black neck-collar. Above black, glossed brown.—*Female*: Brown, neck mottled. No white patch on primaries.

Subfamily Tadorninæ.

Bill more or less raised at base and flattened tip. Plumage more or less rufous. Sexes nearly alike.

Genus **DENDROCYGNA.**

δένδρον = a tree; *κύκνος* = a Swan.

Bill large, long, and of uniform width. Second and third and fourth primaries subequal and longest. No wing-spot.

952. **Dendrocygna javanica.** The Common Whistling Teal.

Soreil, Saral, *Bengal*; **Silli,** *India*; **Chihee,** *Etawah*; **Yerra chilluwa** (Telugu); **Yerreindi,** *Quilon*; **Sisalee,** *Pegu*; **Tingi,** *Manipur.*

♂ 16″ to 18″; 1 to 1¼ lbs. Legs dark. Bill black. Head wood-brown, darkening on to black. Rump and wing-coverts maroon. Lower surface light chestnut.

953. **Dendrocygna fulva.** The Large Whistling Teal.

Murghabi, *Bengal*; **Badak,** *Deccan,* **Yerrinda,** *Travancore*; **Silli,** *India*; **Sisalee,** *Pegu.*

♂ 21″; 1¾ lbs. ♀ 19½″; 1½ lbs. Legs dark. Bill leaden. Head and neck chestnut. In centre of neck a patch of whitish hackles. Flank-feathers long.

Genus **CASARCA.**

Casarca, a proper name = Goose, in South Russian; Tartar *karakchás* = black Goose.

Bill of uniform width, depressed towards tip. Nail large. Brilliant wing-spot.

954. Casarca rutila. THE BRAHMINY DUCK OR RUDDY SHELLDRAKE.

Sarkhab, Chakwa, Chakwi, *India*; **Mungh,** *Sind*; **Sarza,** *Sattara*; **Neer-bathoo,** *S. India*; **Bassana Chilluwa** (Telugu); **Hintha,** *Pegu*; **Surkhed,** *Cabul*; **Hangat,** *Yarkand.*

♂ 24⅛″ to 27″; 3 to 4¼ lbs. ♀ 21¾″ to 24″; 2 to 3¼ lbs. Legs black. Bill black. Neck yellow, with black collar. Upper tail green-black.—*Female* smaller and no collar.

955. Casarca scutulata. THE WHITE-WINGED SHELLDRAKE.

Scŭtŭlata = diamond or lozenge-shaped, chequered.

♂ 28″. Legs black. Bill yellow. Head and neck mottled black and white. Above black-brown. Breast black. (Hume puts these with "*Anas*," H. & M. iii. 147.)

Genus **TADORNA.**

Tadorna, an Italian word, which seems first to occur in Bélon, 1585, as the Latinized name of a bird.

Bill short, high, swelling at base, and concave in middle. Tip flat and turning up. Nail hooked.

956. Tadorna cornuta. THE BURROW DUCK OR COMMON SHELLDRAKE.

Cornūta = horned; from *cornu* = a horn.
Shah-chakwa, *Upper India*; **Niraji,** *Sind*; **Shah moorghabi,** *Cabul.*

♂ 23″ to 25″; 3 lbs. ♀ 21″ to 22″; 2 lbs. Legs red. Bill red, tip black. Brown breast-band, uniting on back. Mesial black line.—*Female*: Lower plumage white, mottled brown; no band.

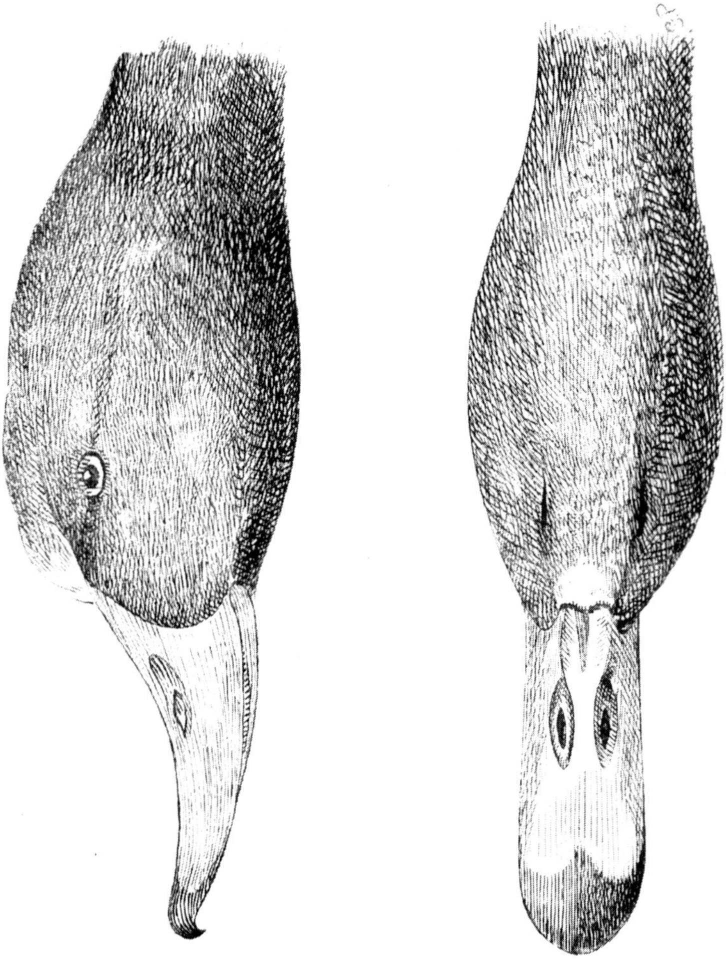

956. *Tadorna cornuta.* Helaya.

Family ANATIDÆ.

Bill broader at base than high, of equal width or wider at tip, with numerous lamellæ. Sexes differ greatly.

Subfamily ANATINÆ. RIVER-DUCKS.

Hind toe not bordered. Bill usually of even width throughout or wider at tip, not raised at base. Numerous fine lamellæ. Rapid flight.

Genus SPATULA.

Spătŭla = a small flat instrument, any thing broad like a spoon, *spătha*.

Bill much dilated. Lamellæ very fine and projecting.

957. Spatula clypeata. THE SHOVELLER.

Clypĕāta = armed with a shield, *clypeus* or *clipeus*; from its white shield-like gorget. **Tidari, Punana,** *N. W. P.*; **Alipat,** *Sind*; **Kanak-aurdak,** *Yarkand.*

♂ 19″ to 22″. ♀ 18″ to 19″. Legs orange. Bill brownish. Head, back, rump, upper and lower tail brown, glossed green. Lesser coverts grey. Speculum bright green.—*Female* dark brown, edged whitish.

Genus ANAS.

νῆττα = a duck, from *νέω* = to swim.

Bill not so deep as wide, of nearly uniform width. Lamellæ short. Nostrils near base of bill.

958. Anas boschas. THE MALLARD OR COMMON WILD DUCK.

Nilsir, *India*; **Lilgah,** *Nepal*; **Niroji,** *Sind*; **Sabz-zurdan,** *Cabul*; **Sun,** *Yarkand.*

♂ 22½″ to 24″; 2½ to 4 lbs. ♀ 20″ to 21½″; 2 to 2½ lbs. Legs orange. Bill yellowish. Head emerald-green. Speculum prussian-blue. Four central tail-feathers curled.—*Female*: Brown, edged lighter. Head and neck yellowish. Fifth remix absent.

959. Anas pœcilorhyncha. THE SPOTTED-BILLED DUCK.

Garmpai, *India*; **Gugral,** *N. W. P.*; **Hunjur,** *Sind*; **Kara,** *Manipur*; **Naddun,** *Nepal.*

♂ 24″ to 26″; 2¼ to 3¼ lbs. ♀ 22″ to 24″; 2 to 2¾ lbs. Sexes alike. Brown eye-line. Speculum green, with black tip, edged white. Greater coverts white, edged deep black.

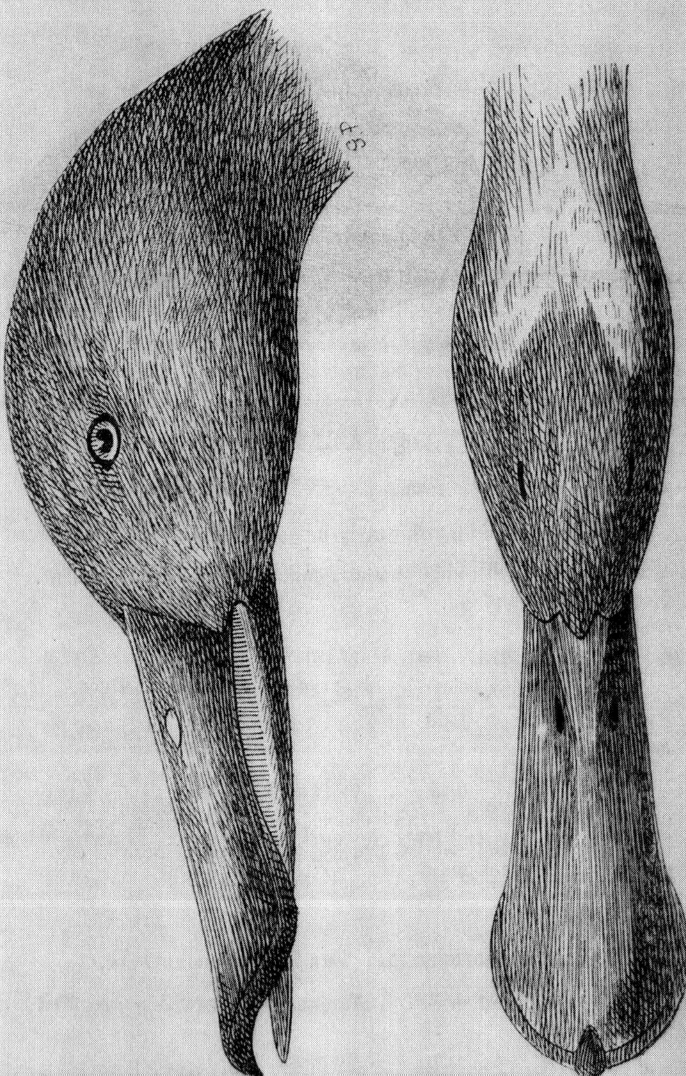

957. *Spatula clypeata.*

958. *Anas boschas.*

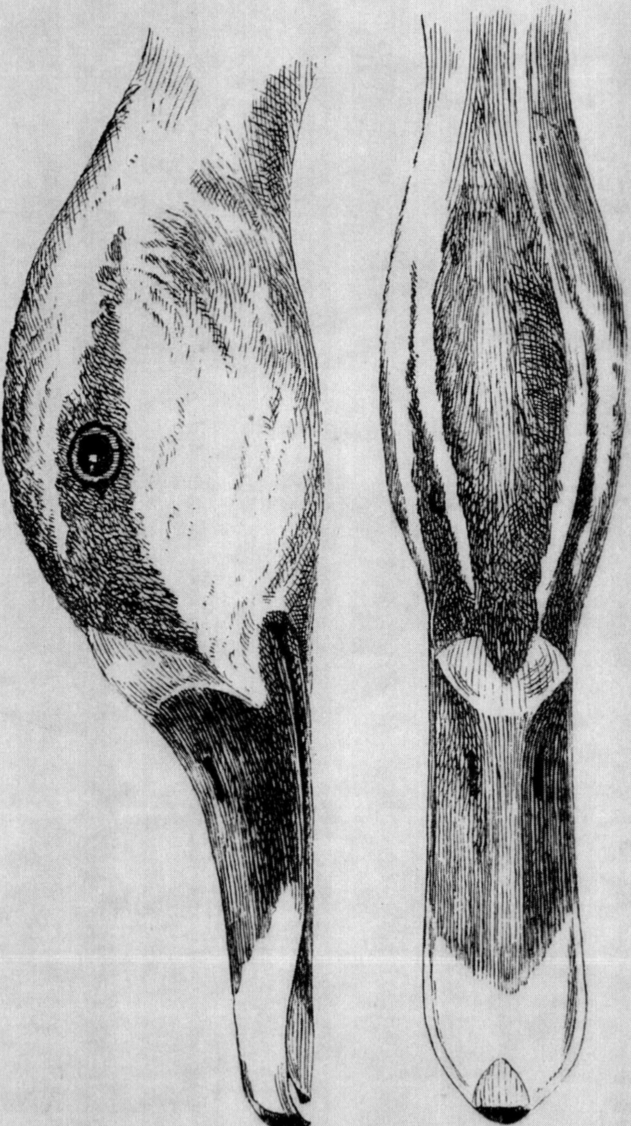

959. *Anas pœcilorhyncha.* Kipling, Lahore, 1876.

960. **Anas caryophyllacea.** THE PINK-HEADED DUCK.

Saknal, *Bengal*; **Lal sira**, *India*; **Doomrar**, *Nepal*; **Doomar**, *Tirhoot.*

♂ 24″. Legs black. Bill rosy, tip bluish. *In summer*: Rosy tuft. Plumage chocolate.—*Female* more dull. Vertex with brown spot.

Genus CHAULELASMUS.

χαυλός = loose, gaping; a word found only in classical Greek, χαυλιόδους = with outstanding teeth; and ἔλασμός = metal beaten out, a metal plate, from ἐλαύνω = I drive, strike, beat out. From the projecting laminæ of the upper mandible.

Bill narrows slightly towards tip. Small nail. Lamellæ long.

961. **Chaulelasmus streperus.** THE GADWALL OR GREY DUCK.

Strĕpĕrus = noisy.
Mila, *India*; **Beykhur**, *N. W. P.*; **Mail**, *Nepal*; **Burd**, *Sind*; **Syah-dum**, *Cabul.*

♂ 20″ to $21\frac{1}{2}$″; $1\frac{1}{2}$ to 2 lbs. ♀ 18″ to 20″; 1 to $1\frac{3}{4}$ lbs. Back brown, with crescent lines. Wing-coverts chestnut. Speculum white and black.—*Female* brown, edged buff. Bill pale, with red margins.

Genus DAFILA.

Tail long, with central tail elongated. Lamellæ not projecting.

962. **Dafila acuta.** THE PIN-TAILED DUCK.

Acūta = sharp, pointed; from *acŭo* = I sharpen.
Sinkpar, *N. W. P.*; **Dighons**, *Bengal*; **Laitunga**, *Manipur*; **Taw-boy**, *Burmah*; **Digoonch**, *Nepal*; **Kokarali**, **Drighush**, *Sind*; **Sink-dum**, *Cabul*; **Chasugshu-aurdah**, *Yarkand.*

♂ 22″ to 29″; $1\frac{3}{4}$ to $2\frac{3}{4}$ lbs. ♀ 20″ to 22″; 1 to 2 lbs. Head umber. White neck-streaks. Speculum green, glossed purple. Long central tail black—*Female* brown, edged white.

Genus MARECA.

Marēca, the native name, according to Marcgrave, of the Brazilian Teal (*Querquedula brasiliensis*).

Bill raised at base, narrowing. Lamellæ project in centre. Short tail cuneate.

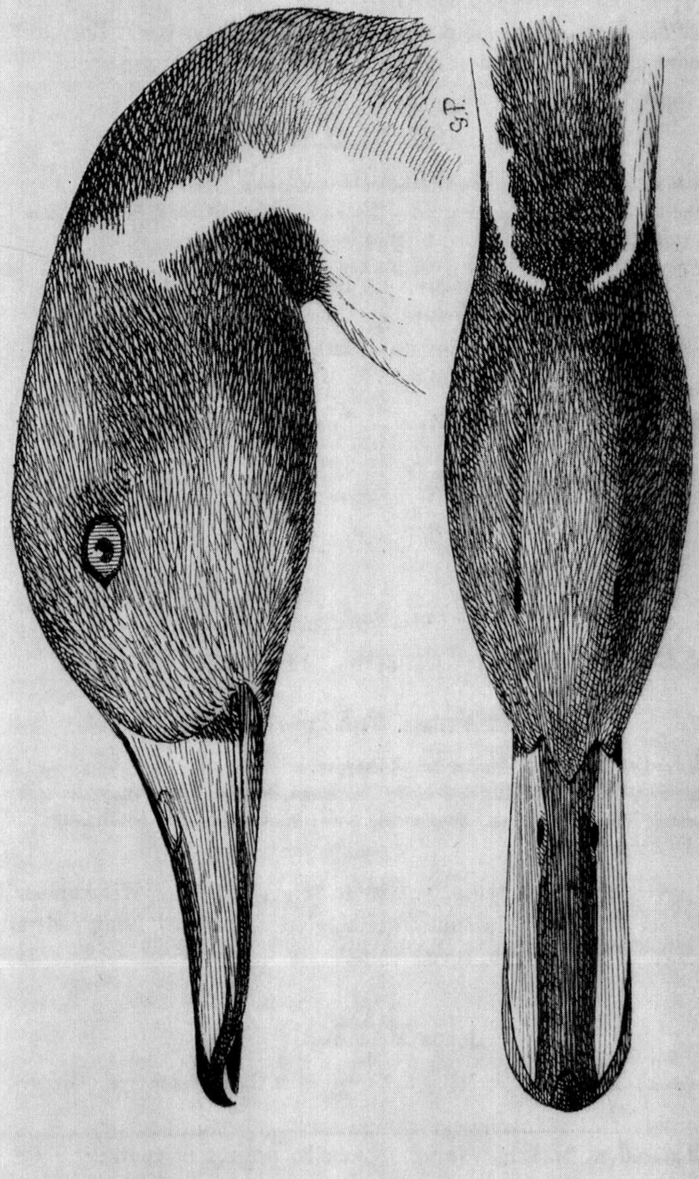

962. *Dafila acuta.*

963. Mareca penelope. The Wigeon or Whew.

Pénélŏpé; πηνέλοψ = a kind of Duck with purple stripes, in classical Greek, which was said to have fed Penelope (subsequently the wife of Ulysses) after her parents had thrown her into the sea.

Pea-san, Patari, *N. W. P.*; **Cheyun,** *Nepal*; **Parow,** *Sind*; **Ade,** *Ratnagiri.*

♂ $19''$ to $19\frac{1}{2}''$; $1\frac{1}{4}$ to $1\frac{1}{2}$ lbs. ♀ $18''$ to $19''$; $1\frac{1}{8}$ to $1\frac{3}{4}$ lbs. Legs

Munchur Lake.

leaden. Bill blue, black tip. Crown yellow. Neck chestnut. Speculum green, bounded above and below with black.—*Female* fulvous. Head speckled.

Genus QUERQUEDULA.

Querquedŭla, a kind of Duck mentioned by Varro and Columella; perhaps from κέρκουρος = a light vessel used by the Cyprians, or from κέρκαιρω = I ring. Professor Skeat says the name is from an onomatopœic base, *querq* or *kark*, significative of any loud noise. According to O. Müller's conjecture, from the Greek κέρκουρος. Hence the French *çerçelle*.

Bill moderate, of uniform width, slightly raised at base. Lamellæ not apparent. Nail small, tip obtuse.

964. Querquedula crecca. THE COMMON TEAL.

Crecca, probably from its note. Cf. *Crex*, q. v., and the German *Kriech-Ente*; old English *Cracker* = Pintail.

Moorghabi, *India*; **Kerra,** *N. W. P.*; **Naroib,** *Bengal*; **Baiji-lagairi,** *Nepal*; **Kardo,** *Sind*; **Killowai,** *Madras*; **Sorlai haki,** *Mysore*; **Churaka,** *Cabul*; **Alah-bash, Kurak-aurdak,** *Yarkand*.

♂ $14\frac{1}{2}''$ to $16''$; 10 to 15 oz. ♀ $13\frac{1}{2}''$ to $15''$; $7\frac{1}{2}$ to 12 oz. Legs greyish. Bill black. Green eye-patch. Head brown. Speculum green, with black sides, with yellow bar above.—*Female*: Throat, cheeks, and eye-band yellow, spotted black.

965. Querquedula circia. THE GARGANEY OR BLUE-WINGED TEAL.

Circia, the ancient name, though not used by any classical author; probably from the root of κίρκος = the Hawk.

Chaitwa, *N. W. P.*; **Ghangroib,** *Bengal*; **Sitch-dum,** *Cabul*; **Karak-aurdak,** *Yarkand*.

♂ $16''$; 10 oz. to 1 lb. ♀ $15''$; 9 to 15 oz. Legs dusky. Bill blackish. White streak over eye. Speculum greyish green, with white bar above and below.—*Female* dusky, edged whitish. Wing-coverts ash-grey.

966. Querquedula formosa. THE BIMACULATED OR CLUCKING-TEAL.

♂ $15\frac{1}{2}''$; 1 lb. Legs dusky. Bill dusky. Head purple, with white eye-line. Black throat-patch. Speculum green, ending velvet-black, bordered silver.—*Female* dusky, edged rufous. Tail-coverts white, with brown spots.

Querquedula falcata. THE CRESTED OR BRONZE-CAPPED TEAL.

♂ $19\frac{3}{4}''$; $1\frac{3}{8}$ lbs. Legs drab. Bill black. Frontal spot white. Head bronze, with green eye-patch. Throat white, with greenish band. Back mottled. (H. & M. iii. 231.)

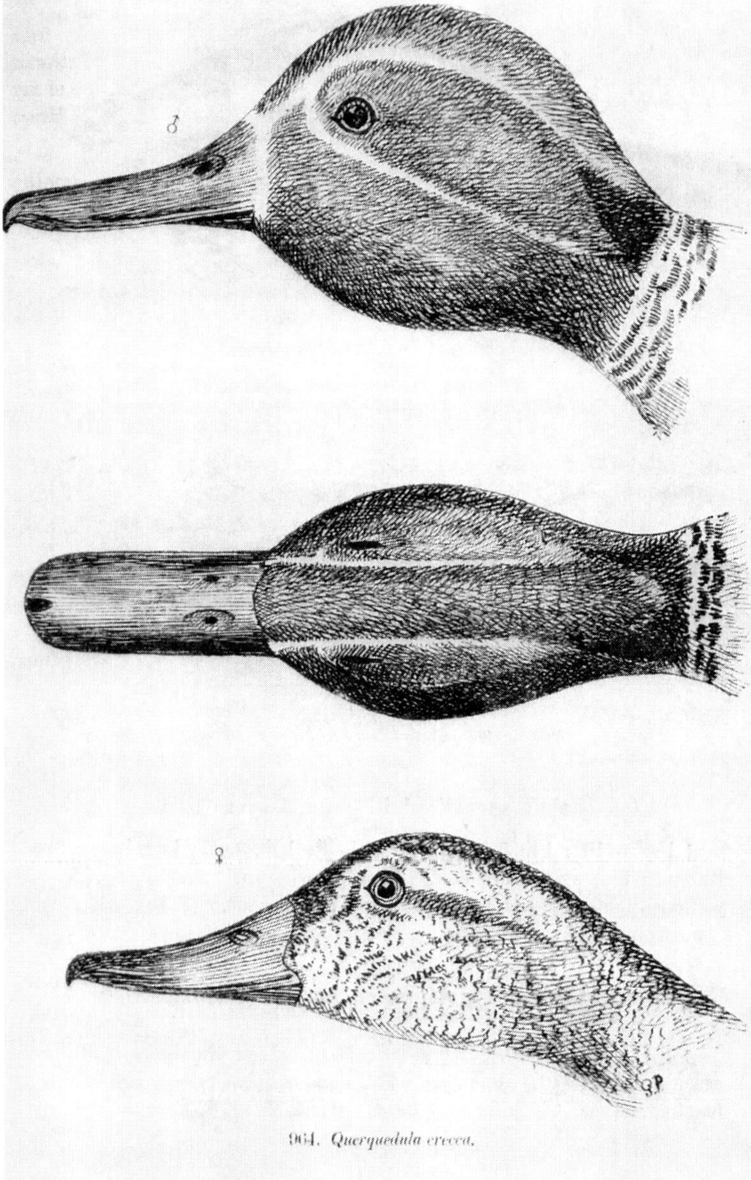

964. *Querquedula crecca.*

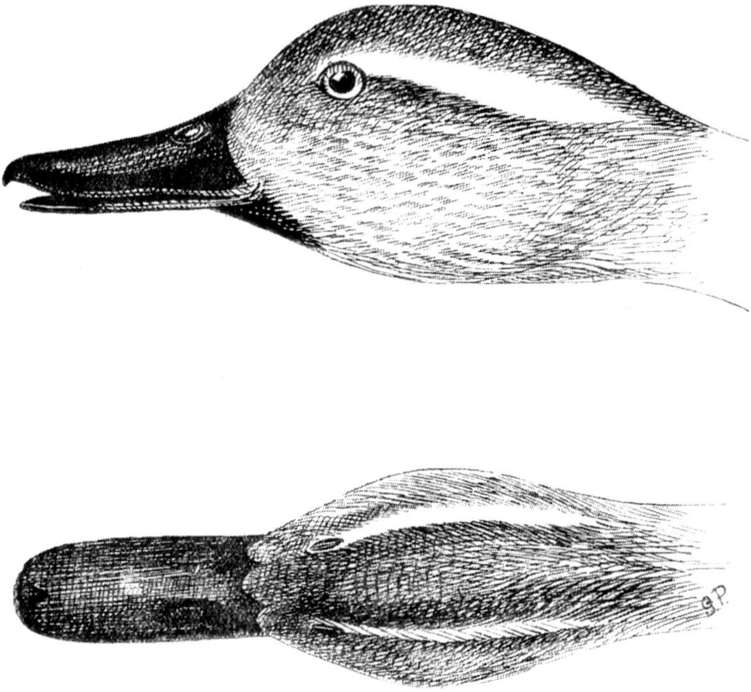

965. *Querquedula circia.*

Querquedula angustirostris. THE MARBLED TEAL.

♂ 18½″ to 19″; 1 lb. 5 oz. ♀ 17″ to 17½″; 1 lb. 3 oz. Legs brown. Bill with blue spot above nail. Back grey-brown. Scapulars with yellowish spots.—*Female*: Eye-patch less conspicuous. (S. F. i. 262.)

Scarcely a *Querquedula*.

Querquedula gibberifrons. THE OCEANIC TEAL.

♂ 16″ to 18″; 1 lb. ♀ 15″ to 16″; 12 oz. Legs plumbeous. Bill greenish. Eye set in white ring. Full short occipital crest. Brilliant longitudinal metallic green wing-band. (H. & M. iii. 243.)

Subfamily FULIGULINÆ. DIVING DUCKS.

Stout heavy body. Coloured in masses. Speculum less plain or wanting. Hind toe short and bordered. Feet large and webbed to the toes.

Genus BRANTA.

Brenta, a mediæval word (*Branta* in Gesner and Aldrovandus). *Brent* = burnt; probably from its generally charred appearance.

Bill long; tip depressed, with rather large nail. Lamellæ distant, large, and prominent.

967. Branta rufina. THE RED-CRESTED POCHARD.

Rūfina, apparently an adjectival form, from *rūfus* = red.

Doomer, *Nepal*; **Rattoba**, *Sind*; **Nool-gool**, *Cabul*; **Kizil-bash aurdak**, *Yarkand*; **Lalsir**, *N. W. P.*

♂ 22″. Legs waxy. Bill red, tip white. Crown-feathers elongated. Neck, breast, and abdomen black. Flanks white. Speculum white.—*Female* on water appears grey, with dark eye-stripe and crest.

Genus AYTHYA.

αἴθυια = a water-bird; perhaps the Solan Goose or Gannet (*Sula alba*).

968. Aythya ferina. THE CANVAS-BACK OR RED-HEADED POCHARD.

Fĕrina = of or belonging to wild animals, *fĕræ*; perhaps in reference to its "game" flavour. *Cf.* German *Tafel-Ente*, "Table-duck."

Lalsir, *N. W. P.*; **Lalmuriya**, *Bengal*; **Chooon**, *Bengal*; **Thadingnam**, *Manipur*; **Rutubah**, *Sind*; **Surkh-sir**, *Cabul.*

♂ 18″ to 18½″; 2 to 2¼ lbs. ♀ 17″ to 18″; 1¼ to 2¼ lbs. Legs bluish. Bill blue; tip and base black. Back white, with black lines. Breast black.—*Female* the same, with breast red-brown, mottled white.

969. Aythya nyroca. THE WHITE-EYED POCHARD.

Nyrŏca, Latinized from the Russian name, *Ootna nyrok.*

Karchiya, *N. W. P.*; **Lalbigri**, *Bengal*; **Burnu**, *Sind*; **Malac**, *Nepal*; **Chiki**, *Yarkand.*

♂ 16″ to 17″; 1⅜ to 1½ lbs. ♀ 15″ to 16½″; 1¼ lbs. Legs grey. Bill bluish. Head and breast red. Collar black. Abdomen white.—*Female* brown, edged pale.

968. *Aythya ferina.*

Genus **FULIGULA.**

Fūlĭgŭla, for *fulicula*, diminutive of *fŭlix* or *Fulica*, q. v. *Fūligo* = soot.

Bill broad throughout; tip broadest. Nostrils advanced.

970. Fuligula marila. THE SCAUP POCHARD.

Marila, from μαρίλη = the embers of charcoal; from its pitch-black fore parts.

♂ 20″. ♀ 19″ to 20″. Legs ashy. Bill blue, black tip. Head, neck, and breast deep black. Speculum, abdomen, and sides white.—*Female* with white eye-space.

971. Fuligula cristata. THE TUFTED POCHARD.

Dubaru, *N. W. P.*; **Malac,** *Nepal*; **Turando,** *Sind*; **Ablak,** *Cabul.*

♂ 16½″ to 17″; 1½ to 2 lbs. ♀ 15″ to 16¾″; 1¼ to 1¾ lbs. Legs

leaden. Bill grey, black tip. Black silky crest. Breast black. Speculum white, with greenish edge.—*Female* spotted beneath.

Genus **CLANGULA.**

Clangŭla, from *clango* = resound, clank; diminutive of *clanga*; κλαγγή = *clangor*, any sharp sound, especially the scream of Cranes.

Head full and puffy. Differ from other Sea-Ducks in preferring fresh water.

Clangula glaucion. THE GARROT OR GOLDEN-EYED POCHARD.

Glaucion = γλαύκιον, a grey-eyed water-bird in Athenæus, 895 B.C.; from γλαυκός = bluish-grey. Generally Latinized into *glaucium* by pre-Linnean writers, and always by botanists, including Linnæus.

♂ 16″ to 19″; 2 to 2½ lbs. ♀ 15½″ to 16½″; 1½ to 2 lbs. Legs yellow. Bill bluish. Head black-green, with black mouth-patch. Neck, breast, and below white. Back black. (H. & M. iii. 285.)

Genus **ERISMATURA.**

Stiff and pointed tail of 18 feathers.

Erismatura leucocephala. THE WHITE-FACED OR SPINY-TAILED POCHARD.

♂ 16½″. Legs plumbeous. Bill plumbeous. Above hair-brown, minutely speckled, fulvous. Below bright orange-fulvous. White stripe from upper mandible to nape. (H. & M. iii. 289.)

Family MERGIDÆ.

Bill cylindrical, edged with teeth; tip well bent over. Head more or less crested.

Genus **MERGUS.**

Mergus, i, m. [*mergo*], a diver; a diving-bird, in classical Latin.

Bill narrow and toothed. Do not acquire full plumage till second autumnal moult. Tail wedge-shaped, of 16 or 18 feathers.

972. Mergus merganser. THE COMMON MERGANSER.

Merganser = a diving Goose; from *mergus* + *anser*. Coined by Gesner, on account of the bird's size.

Ala ghaz aurdak, *Yarkand.*

♂ 25″ to 28″; 2¾ to 3¼ lbs. ♀ 23″ to 25″; 2 to 2¾ lbs. Legs orange. Bill blood-red, with black ridge. Crest, head, and neck glossy green. Above black and ashy. Breast and abdomen white. Wing-coverts orange.—*Female*: Ashy-red head.

972. *Mergus merganser.* Bishop-Charbar, Mekran coast, 29-1-75.

Mergus serrator. The Red-breasted Merganser.

Serrātor = one using a saw, *serra.*

♂ 24″ to 26″; 2 lbs. ♀ 22″ to $23\frac{1}{2}$″. Legs deep red. Bill deep red. Light brown band streaked black round base of neck. Narrow black band down back of neck. Flanks white, vermiculated grey and black. (H. & M. iii. 305.)

Genus MERGELLUS.

Of small size. Pied black and white. Tail of 16 feathers.

973. Mergellus albellus. The Smew or White-headed Merganser.

Albellus = the little white (*albus*) bird.
Nihenne, *Etawah*; **Chota Khoruk,** *Cabul*; **Boz aurdak,** *Yarkand.*

♂ 17″ to 18″; $1\frac{1}{4}$ to $1\frac{3}{4}$ lbs. ♀ $15\frac{1}{2}$″ to $16\frac{3}{4}$″; 1 to $1\frac{1}{2}$ lbs. Legs leaden. Bill bluish. Black eye-patch. Beneath white, with two black bands.—*Female*: Head red-brown. Below clouded ashy.

Tribe *MERGITORES.*

Food chiefly fishes, crustacea, or insects. Bill long, straight, and pointed. Hind toe lobed.

Family COLYMBIDÆ. Imbers, Divers, or Loons.

Peculiar to northern hemisphere. Frequent seas in preference to fresh water. Short tail, and can stand upright.

Inhabit Arctic Circle, migrating southward. Rarely fly. The Great Northern Diver visits England.

Family PODICIPIDÆ.

Feet lobed. Tail almost wanting. Under-plumage silky. Head often tufted.—*Young* striped black and white.

Genus **PODICEPS.**

An ill-formed word, from *pōdex*, gen. *pōdĭcis* = the fundament, and *pēs* = a foot; as if for *podici-pes.*

Bill straight, compressed. Nostrils long. Tarsus with large scutellæ. Hind toe bordered by web.

974. Podiceps cristatus. THE CRESTED GREBE.

♂ 21″ to 24″; $2\frac{1}{2}$ to $3\frac{1}{2}$ lbs. ♀ 20″; $2\frac{1}{4}$ lbs. Legs leaden. Bill

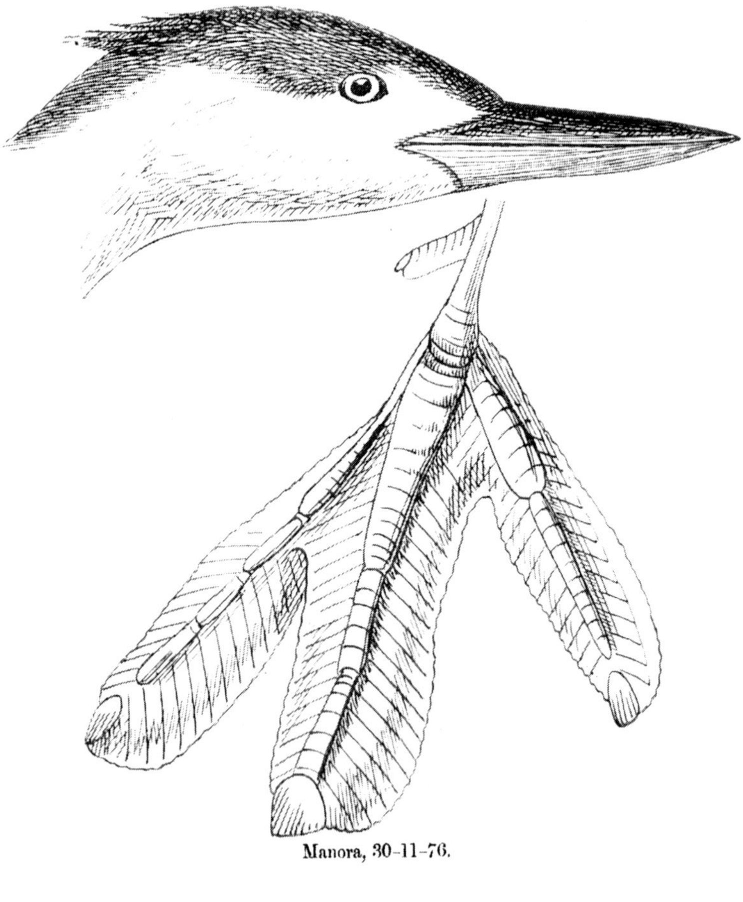

Manora, 30-11-76.

brown, tip white. Double black crest. Red-and-black collar.—*Young*: No crest and collar rusty.

Podiceps nigricollis.

With black neck; from *niger* + *collum*.

♂ 13″; 1 lb. ♀ 12″. Legs greenish. Bill black.—*In summer*: Broad streak of orange behind eye. Sides and flanks streaked orange. —*In winter*: Eye-tuft wanting. (S. F. i. 266.)

975. Podiceps minor. THE DABCHICK OR LITTLE GREBE.

Panturri, Churaka, *India*; **Dubari,** *Bengal*; **Manu-gudi-kodi** (Telugu).

♂ 8″ to 9″. Legs greenish. Bill black. Chin black. Cheeks, ear-coverts, and sides of neck bright chestnut. Above black, tinged green.

Tribe *VAGATORES.*

Food chiefly fishes, crustacea, or insects. Bill hooked at tip or pointed. Wings long and pointed.

LAND BIRDS are only at sea by accident. COAST BIRDS are seen at sea, but near land. OCEAN BIRDS seldom visit shore, except to breed. Land Birds explain wind-currents, while difference between Coast and Ocean Birds is the difference between signs that do and signs that do not prove proximity of land. As a rough distinction, the more a bird lives on land the more he flaps his wings. The Rook flaps continually. The Gull skims and flaps in about equal ratio. The Albatross rarely, if ever, flaps.

Family PROCELLARIDÆ.

Bill hooked, and appears as if joined. Nostrils contained in one tube.

Subfamily DIOMEDINÆ. ALBATROSSES.

Of large size, and known in flight by the white of underwing, with hindmost edge of white or brown.

Of Albatrosses proper there are two types. *Diomedea fuliginosa*, the Great Albatross, brown all over, speckled white. Stretch of wing 10 to

14 feet; one has been measured 17 feet. In life beak is pink, and cheeks streaked rose. Most clumsy on the water, and very timid in approaching anything that moves. Name probably a composition of Arabic-Portuguese "Alcatraz," meaning any big sea-bird.

Rarely, if ever, seen within the tropics. Common in Great Southern Ocean, and, curiously enough, though frequent in Behring Strait, it is practically unknown in the North Atlantic. The Albatross supports 20 lbs. weight on an area of 16 s. f. of wing for hours together without any apparent effort, crossing and recrossing wake of ship steaming 16 miles an hour, and all this with wings perfectly still, except for an occasional flap, say three or four times an hour. The "Molly-Mauk."

D. chlororhynchos is distinguished by black on top of wings continued across body. ('Illustrated Guide Orient Line.')

Subfamily PROCELLARINÆ.

Procellāria, procĕlla, æ, f. = storm, tempest.

Hind toe generally present. Almost black. Nostrils in a tube.

There are varieties of Petrel between the Cape and Australia, ranging between the Cape Dove and True Albatross. All of uniform dark hue. Sailors call them generally "Stink-pots" and "Cape Hens," and the special epithet "Parsons" is given to a lesser species with white bill and white spectacles. To the larger, with greenish beak, the terms "Nelly" or "Mother Carey's Goose" are applied: this is the Sooty Petrel (*D. spadiceus*), and it is the Petrel that most frequently soars over deck, and may be shot so as to fall on board.

Genus **DAPTION.**

δάπτω = I devour.

Long wings. Short tail. Small feet. Bill short, thick, and well hooked at tip. Lower mandible truncated. Few lamellæ on inner margin of upper mandible.

Daption capensis. THE CAPE PIGEON OF FLYING PETREL.

(Called also "Pintado Petrel.")

Has a spread of wing $2\frac{1}{2}$ feet.

♂ 14 to 18 oz. Legs dark brown. Bill blackish. Head, above, and primaries soot-brown. Wing-coverts, back, and upper tail white, each feather tipped soot-brown. Below white. Small white streak below eye. (S. F. vii. 442.)

The "Cape Dove" or "Fulmer Petrel" is larger, and known as the "Mall Duck."

Genus **PRION.**

πρίων = a saw, jagged, serrated.

Neat plumage. Weak bill. Lamellæ in upper mandible. Colour blue-grey and white.

Prion ——? THE BLUE PETREL.

Called by sailors "The Whale-Bird." (S. F. ii. 317.)

Genus **THALASSIDROMA.**

θάλασσα = the sea; δρομάω = I run.

Of small size. Slender compressed bill.

It is from the Stormy Petrel (*Thalassidroma*), "Mother Carey's Chicken," that the whole tribe derive their name.

976. Thalassidroma wilsoni. WILSON'S STORM-PETREL.

♂ $7\frac{1}{8}''$. Legs black. Bill black. Pale yellow patch in centre of webs. Second quill longest. Tiny spur at base of tarsus. General plumage sooty. Upper and under tail-coverts white.

Subfamily PUFFININÆ.

Bill arched, hooked. Nostrils tubular, with two openings.

Genus **PUFFINUS.**

Puffinus, the Latinized form of the English "Puffin;" from "to puff" = to blow in an intermittent way, thence "to swell," French "bouffer"; from the swollen bill of *Fratercula arctica*. Brisson seems to have applied the name to the Shearwater, from Willughby calling it the "Puffin of the Isle of Man."

Puffinus persicus. THE SHEARWATER OR PUFFIN PETREL.

♂ 13″ to 14″. Legs white. Bill pale lavender. White line round eye. Lateral lower tail-coverts deep brown. (S. F. i. 5.)

Subfamily Halodrominæ.

Under bill truncated. Nostrils contiguous.

Genus **PELECANOIDES.**

Chin with pouch. No hind claw.

977. Pelecanoides urinatrix. The Little Diving Petrel.

♂ 8½″. Legs greenish. Bill black. Above brown. Chin black. Below white.

Family LARIDÆ. Gulls &c.

Nostrils linear and basal. Hind toe generally present. Plumage grey and white or black and brown.

Subfamily Lestridinæ.

Bill short, thick, and hooked. Tail cuneate and long. Strong sharp claws.

Genus **LESTRIS.**

ληστρίς = a pirate.

Base of bill covered by cere. Two central tail-feathers elongated. First quill longest.

Lestris pomatorhinus. The Pomatorhine Skua.

Pōmătŏrhinus, from πῶμα, genitive πώματος = a lid or cover; ῥίς, genitive ῥινός = the nose, nostril, from the nasal operculum. Originally written *pomarinus*.

♂ 20″. Legs blackish. Bill horny. Crown and nape brown. Chin white. Above deep brown. Primaries with white shafts. Breast-markings deep brown.

Lestris parasiticus. Buffon's Skua.

Parasiticus = παρασιτικός, parasitic, from παράσιτος = one who eats uninvited at the table of another; from παρά = beside, and σῖτος = wheat, food, &c.

♂ 19″; 1 lb. 3 oz. Legs black. Bill brown, yellow cere. Central tail with two broad bars, projects ¾″. Head pale brown, with streaks. Breast white. Flanks white, with bars.

Subfamily LARINÆ.

Bill stout, curved at tip. Wings long. Tail full, even, rounded, or slightly forked. Claws slightly hooked.

Genus LARUS.

λάρος = a ravenous sea-bird, in classical Greek. Akin to Old Norse *liri* = a Tern.

Bill long and strong. Wings long, exceeding tail. No summer hood. Head and neck white.—*In winter*: Streaked brown.

(i.) *Primaries black to their base.*

978. Larus fuscus. THE LESSER BLACK-BACKED GULL.

♂ 24″. Legs dull yellow. Bill citron, red below. Head, neck, and tail white. Body grey-black. First quill, and sometimes second, black, with white spot. Secondaries bordered white. Scapulars black, tipped white.

(ii.) *Primaries greyish towards base.*

Larus cachinnans. THE EASTERN HERRING-GULL.

♂ 23″ to 25¾″; 1¾ to 2 lbs. 6 oz. Legs pale yellow. Bill yellow, red below. Head, neck, tail, and below white. Mantle, secondaries, and tertiaries grey. First quill black, with white band. Second similar, but often without white band.—*In winter*: Spots near tips of bill. (S. F. i. 270.)

Larus affinis.

♂ 24″ to 24½″; 2 to 2¾ lbs. ♀ 22″ to 23½″; 2 lbs. Legs pinkish. Bill yellow, patch red. Same as *L. argentatus*, but mantle and both webs of primaries at base slate-grey. (S. F. i. 273.)

Larus gelastes.

♂ 17½″ to 18¼″; 12 to 14 oz. ♀ 16¾″ to 17¼″; 10 to 11 oz. Legs deep red. Bill deep red. Breast rosy. Mantle French grey. First quill white, tip black, and no black margin on inner web. (S. F. i. 274.)

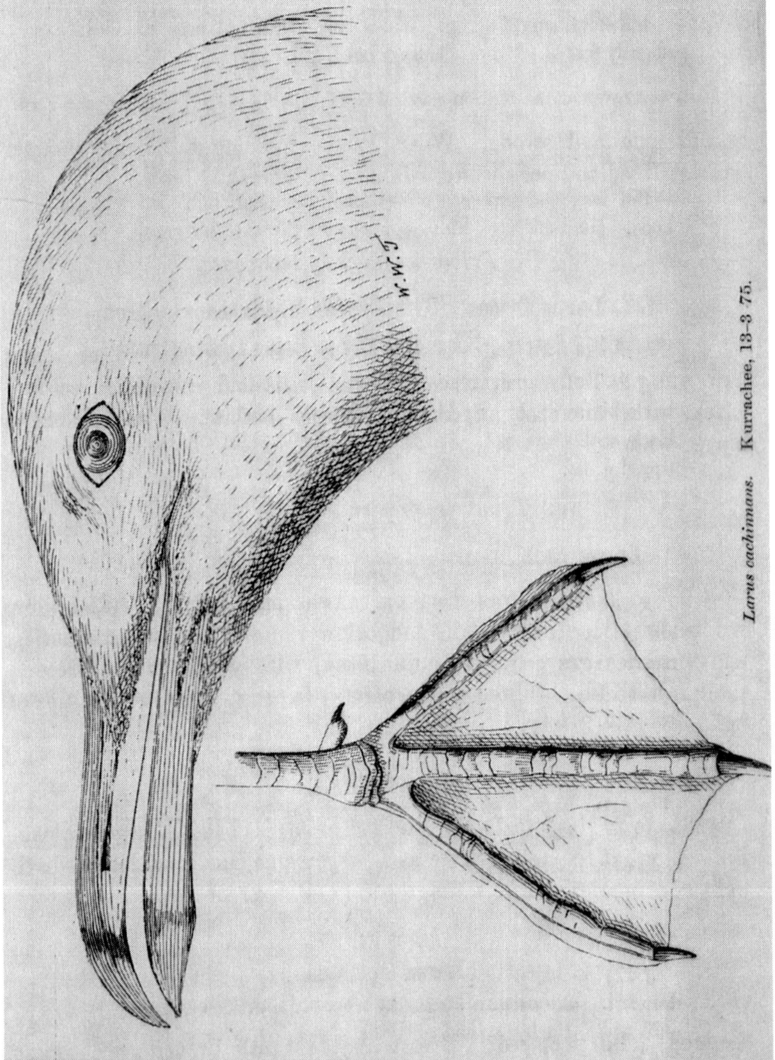

Larus cachinnans. Kurrachee, 13-3-75.

Larus gelastes.

Genus **CHROICOCEPHALUS.**

Summer hood black or brown. Bill strongly hooked.

979. Chroicocephalus ichthyaëtus. THE GREAT BLACK-HEADED GULL.

Fish-eyed, from ἰχθύς + ἀετός.

♂ $29\frac{1}{4}''$; 2 lbs. Legs dull red. Bill red, black bar. Back and wings blue-grey. Five primaries white, with black band. First quill, outer and half inner web, black.

Genus **XEMA.**

A fancy name, apparently devoid of meaning.

Summer hood black or brown. Of small size. Bill rather short. Wings long. Tail short. A very doubtful genus, scarcely admitted by any one.

980. Xema brunneicephala. THE BROWN-HEADED GULL.

♂ 16″ to 17″. Legs red. Bill red, tip dark. Head and neck sooty. Back and wings grey. First quill black, inner web white at base.—*In winter*: Head white, with spot behind ear. Spots on first and second primaries.

981. Xema ridibunda. THE LAUGHING GULL.

Ridibunda = full of laughter; from *rīdĕo* = I laugh.

♂ 15″ to 16″. Legs deep red. Bill deep red. Head and neck red-

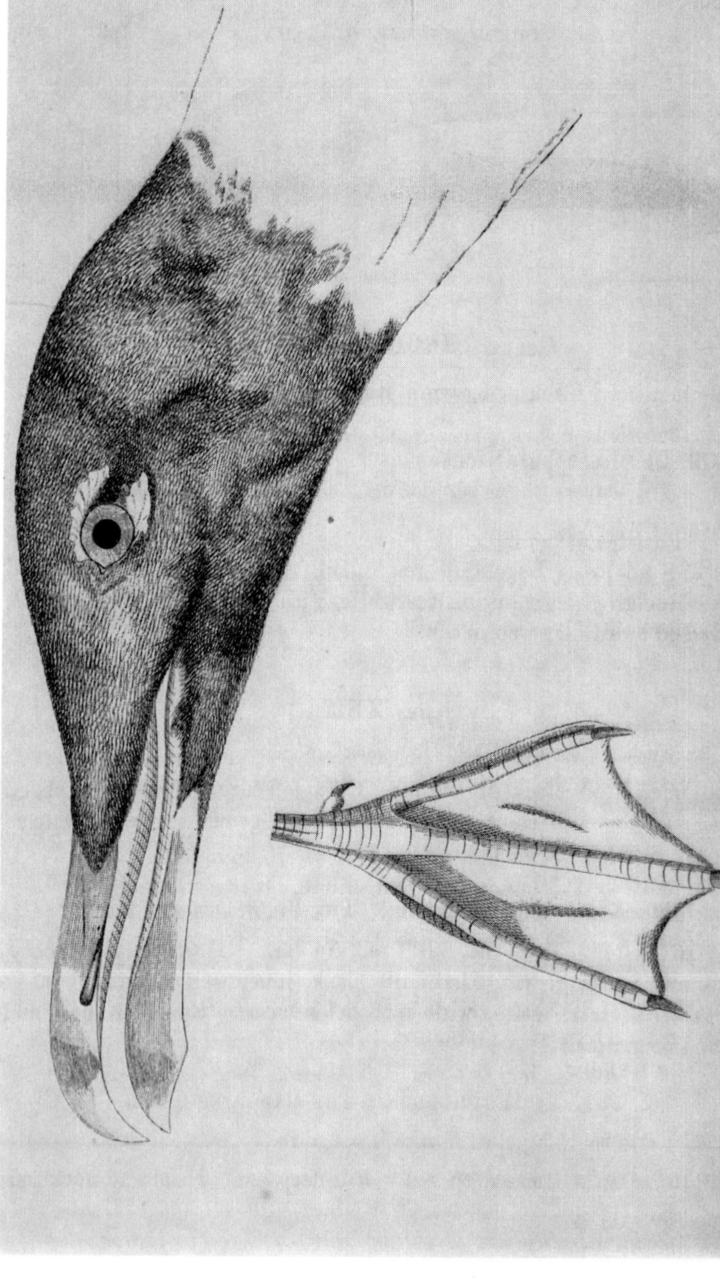

979. *Chroicocephalus ichthyaëtus.* Bishop-Pusnee, Mekran Coast, 7-2-75. Weight 3¾ lbs.

brown. Four quills white. First primary, outer web black, and black margin on inner web.—*In winter*: Head dusky white. First four primaries white, tipped and edged black within.

980. *Xema brunneicephala.* Manora, 3-3-75.

981. *Xema ridibunda.*

Xema melanocephala.

Mĕlănŏcephăla = black-headed; from *μέλας* + *κεφăλή*.

♂ 15″ to 16″. Primaries white, except outer web of first quill. (S. F. i. 278.)

Xema hemprichi. HEMPRICH'S GULL.

♂ $18\frac{3}{4}''$ to $19\frac{1}{4}''$; 14 to 18 oz. ♀ 13 to 14 oz. Legs greenish.

Bill green, tip red. Head grey-brown. Mantle sooty. Quills black, with white tip and spot. (S. F. i. 279.)

Xema minuta. THE SMALL GULL.

♂ $10\frac{1}{4}''$.—*In summer*: Head and neck black.—*In winter*: Head streaked, with spot under eye and behind ear.

Subfamily STERNINÆ. TERNS &c.

Bill almost straight. Long pointed wing. Toes short. Web usually scalloped.

(i.) *Bill Gull-like. Tail shortish.*

Genus **SYLOCHELIDON.**

σύλον = rapine; χελῖδών = a Swallow.

Bill stout and deep. Tail emarginate. Largest of all Terns.

982. Sylochelidon caspia. THE CASPIAN MARSH-TERN.

♂ $18''$ to $20''$. Legs black. Bill coral-red. Head and nape black. Above pearl-grey. Back, neck, and below white. Some primaries edged and tipped.—*In winter*: Head white, with black streaks.

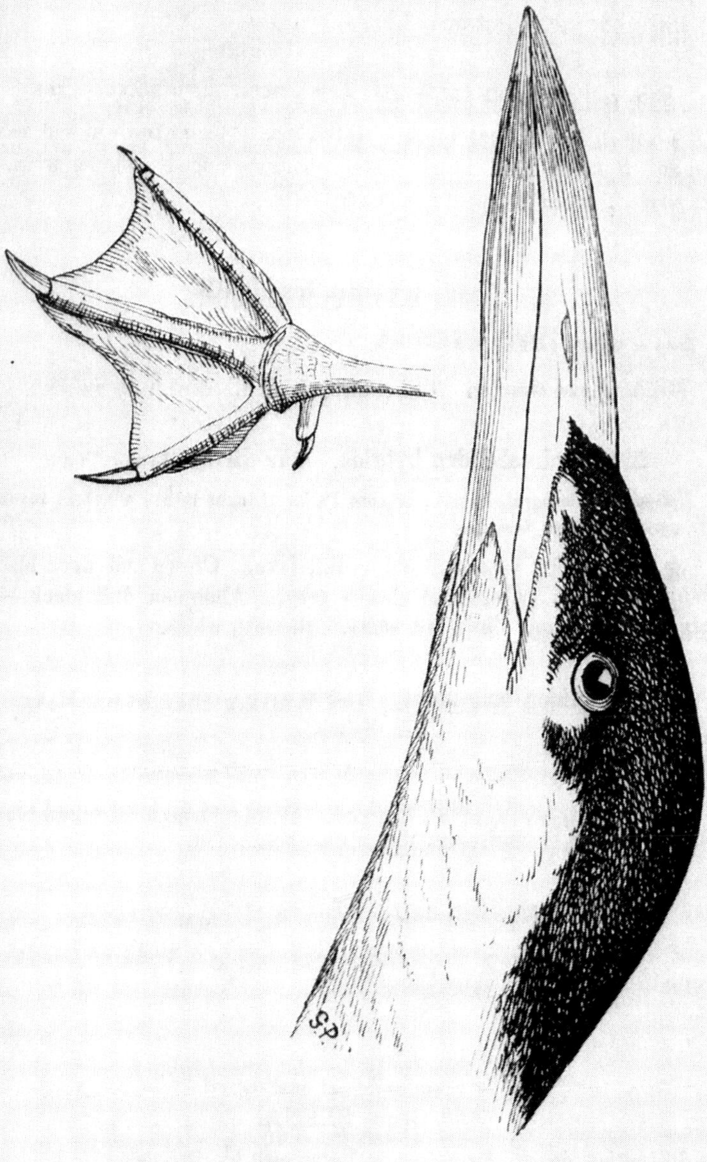

982. *Sylochelidon caspia.* 3–4–75.

Genus **GELOCHELIDON.**

γελάω = I laugh; χελιδών = a Swallow.

Bill moderate. Tail forked.

983. Gelochelidon anglicus. The Gull-billed Marsh-Tern.

♂ 14″ to 16″. Legs black. Bill black. Front, crown, and nape black. Sides of head white. Five primaries tipped on inner webs.—*In winter*: Head white, streaked grey.

Genus **HYDROCHELIDON.**

ὕδωρ = water; χελιδών = a Swallow.

Bill long and slender. Tail slightly forked. Not fully webbed.

984. Hydrochelidon hybrida. The Small Marsh-Tern.

Hybrida = a mongrel, hybrid; because Pallas thought it like a hybrid between *H. nigra* and *Sterna fluviatilis*.

♂ 10″ to 11″. Legs dull red. Bill lake. Crown and nape black. White eye-line. Chin and cheeks grey. Abdomen dull black.—*In winter*: Front and round bill white. Beneath white.

Hydrochelidon leucoptera. The White-winged Black Marsh-Tern.

Leucoptĕra = λευκόπτερος, white-winged; from λευκός + πτερόν.

♂ 10″. Legs red. Bill blackish. Head and neck all round black. Shoulders and greater parts of coverts white.

Hydrochelidon nigra. The Black Marsh-Tern.

♂ 9″. Legs dark red-brown. Bill black. Head and neck all round sooty black. Wings lead-grey.

(ii.) *Slender bodies and forked tail.*

Genus **SEENA.**

Bill stout, deep. Feet short. Inner web $\frac{1}{2}$″.

985. **Seena aurantia.** THE LARGE RIVER-TERN.

Mullcokwalla, 19–10–72.

♂ 15″ to 16″. Legs red. Bill deep yellow. Lateral tail white. Flanks ashy.—*In winter*: Head with white streaks.

Genus **STERNA.**

The Latinized form of the name. Cf. Frisian *Stirn*, German *Tänner*, Swedish *Fisk-tärna*, Norwegian *Makrel-tern*, our *Tern* and *Tarney*. Derivation unknown.

Bill slender, lengthened. Tail much forked.

Sterna dougalli. THE ROSEATE TERN.

In honour of Dr. MacDougall, of Glasgow, who first sent a specimen and description to Montagu in 1812.

♂ $15\frac{4}{5}''$. Legs coral. Bill black. Black head and long, pointed, velvet-black crest. Beneath rose. (S. F. iii. 376.)

986. **Sterna fluviatilis.** THE EUROPEAN OR COMMON RIVER-TERN.

♂ $12\frac{1}{2}''$. Legs red. Bill deep red. Black markings on bill near tip. Wings reaching beyond tail. Tail-feathers white on inner webs. Abdomen greyish.—*In winter*: Crown white.

Sterna longipennis.

Close to the Arctic Tern, *S. hirundo*; but has a slightly longer wing and stronger bill, which is black at all ages. (S. F. iv. 472.)

987. Sterna melanogastra. THE BLACK-BELLIED RIVER-TERN.

♂ 12″. Legs vermilion. Bill orange. Breast pearl-grey. Abdomen brown-black.—*In winter*: Head dusky. Abdomen grey.

Sterna albigena.

♂ $14\frac{1}{2}$″. Legs Indian red. Bill blackish. Patch in front of eye. Back, scapulars, wings, and tail French grey. First primary with large portion of inner web white to margin.

Genus STERNULA.

Head slightly crested.

988. Sternula minuta. THE SMALL RIVER-TERN.

♂ 8″ to $8\frac{1}{2}$″. Legs orange. Bill yellow, black tip. Rump, upper tail-coverts, and tail white. Shafts of outer primaries dark. Crown, eye-line, nape, and hind neck black.

Sternula sinensis.

♂ 10″. Bill yellow, tip black. Shafts of outer primaries white. Rump, tail-coverts, and tail white. (S. F. v. 325.)

Sternula saundersi.

♂ $9\frac{1}{10}$″. Legs yellowish olive. Bill yellow, tip dusky. First three primaries black, with black shafts and broad white margins to inner webs. Rump, tail-coverts, and tail grey. Back grey. Triangular frontal patch. Crown velvet-black.

Sternula gouldi.

♂ $8\frac{1}{10}$″; $1\frac{1}{4}$ oz. Legs dusky orange. Bill green-yellow.

(iii.) *Long wings. Tail forked.*

Genus THALASSEUS.

θαλάσσιος = belonging to the sea.

Bill long and slender. Feet fully webbed. Wings exceeding or equal to forked tail.

989. *Thalasseus cristatus.*

989. Thalasseus cristatus. THE LARGE SEA-TERN.

♂ $19\frac{1}{2}''$ to $21''$; 14 oz. to 1 lb. ♀ 14 oz. to 1 lb. Legs black. Bill pale yellow. Long black crest. Face, nape, and below silky white. Tips of secondaries white.

Thalasseus cantiacus. THE SANDWICH SEA-TERN.

♂ 17″ to 18″; 14 oz. ♀ 16″ to 17″; 12 oz. Legs black. Bill

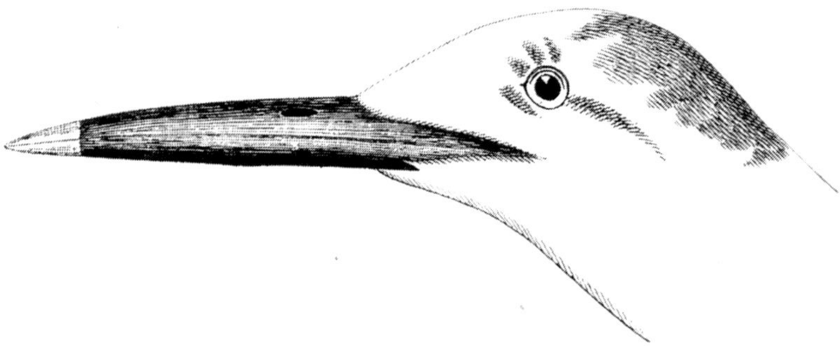

black. Crest black. Lower parts rosy.—*In winter*: Black crescent in front of eye. No rosy hue.

990. Thalasseus bengalensis. THE SMALLER SEA-TERN.

♂ 15″ to 16″. Legs black. Bill yellow. Crest black. Lower parts white. Quills dark grey, with white on inside of inner webs.

Thalasseus alba. THE WHITE SEA-TERN.

Legs orange. Bill black. Snow-white plumage. Only shafts of quills blackish. Rather large bill, conical, pointed, and slightly bent up. Tail graduated.

(iv.) *Plumage more or less black.*

Genus **ONYCHOPRION.**

ὄνυξ, ὄνυχος = a claw; πρίων = a saw.

Tail slightly forked. Middle toe with claw serrated.

991. Onychoprion melanauchen. THE BLACK-NAPED OCEAN-TERN.

♂ 12″. Legs black. Bill black, red tip. Head white. Eye-line widening to nape, black. First quill dark grey on outer web.

992. Onychoprion anasthætus. THE BROWN-WINGED OCEAN-TERN.

♂ 14″. Legs coral-red. Bill dusky red. Crown black. Nape white. Quills blackish.

Onychoprion fuliginosa. THE SOOTY TERN.

♂ 17¾″. ♀ 16″. Legs purplish. Bill purplish. Middle claw much curved. Forehead, chin, neck below, axillaries, wing-lining, and lower tail-coverts white. Nape velvet-black. Back dusky brown.

Genus ANOÜS.

Anŏüs = ἄνοος (trisyllable), without understanding (*νόος, νοῦς*), foolish.

Bill, tip curved slightly up. Nostrils in groove. Tail slightly rounded.

993. Anoüs stolidus. THE COMMON NODDY.

♂ 14″ to 16½″. Sooty brown entirely. Quills and tail darker.

994. Anoüs tenuirostris. THE WHITE-HEADED NODDY.

♂ 11″ to 12″. Legs black. Bill black. Sooty brown. Front and crown white.

Anoüs leucocapillus. (S. F. ii. 322.)

Genus RHYNCHOPS.

ῥύγχος = a bill, *ὤψ* = a face.

Upper mandible much shorter than lower. Both tips of bill truncated.

995. Rhynchops albicollis. THE INDIAN SCISSOR-BILL.

♂ 16½″. Legs vermilion. Bill orange. Head, neck, and central tail black. Lower parts and tail white.—*Young* have bill and feet dusky.

(B) *The young requiring to be fed for a time.*

Tribe *PISCATORES.*

Food chiefly fishes, crustacea, or insects. Feet entirely webbed. Hind toe joined to inner front toe by web. Legs short.

The Tropic-birds, Boobies, Frigate-birds, Pelicans, Cormorants, and Darters are split up by Jerdon into separate families; they might all be included in one family *Pelecanidæ*, and, as all the toes are united by a swimming-membrane, the term (or tribe) *Piscatores* may be considered as equivalent to *Totipalmatæ*.

Family PHAËTONIDÆ. Flying Fishers.

Central tail-feathers very long. Bill finely dentated.

Genus **PHAËTON.**

φαετόντις, poetical feminine of φαέθων = shining.

Toes webbed to the tip. Wings very long. Bill straight, curved on top. Margin of bill finely dentated.

996. Phaëton rubricauda. The Red-tailed Tropic-bird.

♂ 24″ to 25″; 1 to 1¼ lb. ♀ 1 lb. 6 oz. Legs red. Bill red. Silky white, with pink gloss.—*Young* with upper plumage black arrow-marked.

Phaëton indicus. The Boatswain.

(Called also "Tropic-bird" and "Straw-tail.")

♂ 18″, and including two long (much prized) central tail-feathers 20½″; 1½ lbs. ♀ 20¾″. Legs white, claws black. Bill dull orange-red. Black crescent in front of eye. Narrow black line from gape to nostrils and from nostrils to culmen, dividing feathers from bill. First five primaries black. Back, scapulars, rump, and upper tail-coverts white, regularly and closely barred black.

997. Phaëton candidus. The White Tropic-bird.

♂ 29″. Legs dusky. Bill yellow. White, with black wing-band. Tail white, stem black.

Family SULIDÆ. Plunging Fishers.

Bill stout. Tail wedged.

Genus **SULA.**

Latinized from the Norse *Sule*, which is said to mean an awkward fellow, a dolt.

Upper mandible furrowed. Nostrils minute, in long groove. Tail wedge-shaped.

998. **Sula fiber.** The Common Booby.

♂ 26″ to 29″. Above dark brown. Underparts white.—*Young* all brown.

999. **Sula piscator.** The White Booby.

♂ 26″ to 27″. Legs red. Bill red. Upper tail slightly mottled. Wings and tail dusky.

Sula cyanops.

♂ 33″. ♀ 32″. Legs lavender. Bill bluish. Tail, quills, and greater wing-coverts black. (S. F. v. 303.)

Family ATTAGENIDÆ. Pouncing Fishers.

Bill long; both mandibles bent downwards.

Genus **ATTAGEN.**

ἀττάγας = a long-billed bird fond of the water.

Bill long, hooked, and bent down. Long tail forked.

1000. **Attagen aquilus.** The Common Frigate-bird.

(Sometimes called "Sea-Hawk," "Man-of-War Bird," and might also be called a "Gannet-Eagle.")

♂ 37″. Legs red. Bill red. Glossy black.—*Young* with head, neck, and abdomen white.

Attagen minor. The Little Frigate-bird.

♂ 33″. Legs dusty yellow. Bill red. Head and above ferruginous brown. Throat and breast white. Tail greatly forked. (S. F. vii. 447.)

Family PELECANIDÆ. Swimming Fishers.

Huge bill, with pouch.

Genus PELECANUS.

πελέκανος = a Byzantine form of πελεκάν, a bird known to the Greeks, a Woodpecker; from πέλεκυς = an axe.

Nostrils concealed in a groove extending throughout bill. Two bony arches support a huge extensive pouch. Of gigantic size.

(i.) *Frontal plumes come to a point.*

1001. Pelecanus onocrotalus. The European or White Pelican.

Ŏnŏcrŏtălus = ὀνοκρόταλος, the Pelican, in Pliny; from ὄνος = an ass, and κρότἄλον = a rattle.

♂ 68″; 25 lbs. Legs fleshy. Bill 16″, with crimson central line. Primaries and winglet black. Secondaries have outer webs white and inner webs grey. Small crest. Pouch yellow, mixed red and purple.

Pelecanus longirostris.

♂ 54″. Legs reddish. General colour dull white. Primaries, greater coverts, winglet, and secondaries deep brown. All secondaries silvered on outer web. Tail white, freckled and mottled dusky. Foreneck, breast, and abdomen intermingled buff. (S. F. v. 491.)

1002. Pelecanus mitratus. The Crested Pelican.

♂ 62″. Legs flesh-red. Bill 15½″, yellow, tip red. Crest 5″ long. Primaries dusky. Secondaries grey on outer and black on inner web. Pouch yellow.

1003. Pelecanus javanicus. The Lesser White Pelican.

♂ 56″. Legs flesh-pink. Bill 13″. Centre blue, tip red. Tertiaries whitish, with broad black margins. Breast-feathers of some birds golden.

(ii.) *Frontal plumes square.*

1004. Pelecanus philippensis. THE GREY PELICAN.

♂ 62″. Legs fleshy. Bill blue, tip yellow. Slight crest slightly recurved. Primaries dusky, with black shafts. Lower feathers lanceolate white, with grey margins.

Pelecanus crispus.

♂ 62½″. Silver-white. Crest lengthened and recurving. (S. F. i. 110.)

Family GRACULIDÆ. DIVING FISHERS.

Bill cylindric, hooked, and grooved. Tail stiff. Plumage black.

Genus GRACULUS.

Grăcŭlus = a Jackdaw, in classical Latin; akin to *garrio* = I chatter, *gallus* = a cock.

Bill, tip well hooked. Nostrils narrow. Under mandible truncated. Cuneate tail.

(i.) *Tail of* 14 *feathers.*

1005. Graculus carbo. THE LARGE CORMORANT.

Carbo = a coal; perhaps from the bird's sooty blackness.

♂ 32″ to 34″. Legs black. Bill brownish. General colour bronze, with black edges. White spot on thigh-coverts.—*In summer*: Neck-feathers white and hair-like.

1006. Graculus sinensis. THE LESSER CORMORANT.

♂ 24″ to 27″. Legs black. Bill brown, red below. Cheeks pale brown. Bronze feathers as in *G. carbo*.—*In summer*: White ear-tufts. Chin black.

(ii.) *Tail of* 12 *feathers.*

1007. Graculus javanicus. THE LITTLE CORMORANT.

♂ 19″ to 20″. Legs black. Bill brown. Feathers black, edged brown. Chin white.—*In summer*: Short crest and white triangle on crown.

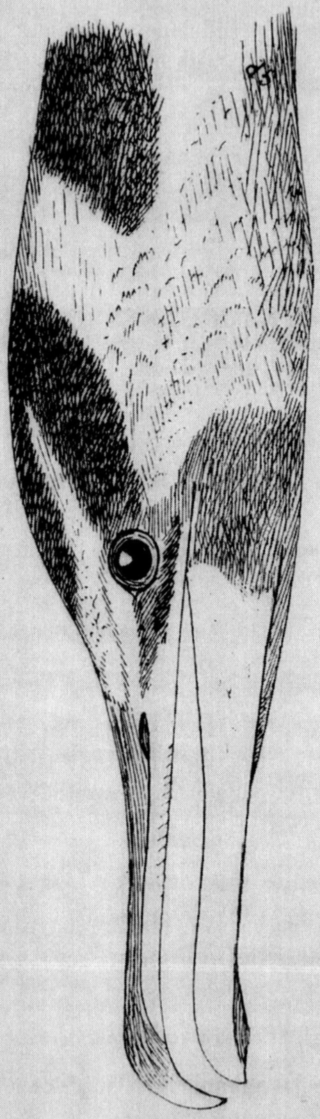

1005. *Graculus carbo.*

Subfamily PLOTINÆ. DARTERS.

Bill long, slender, and acute. Margins finely serrated. Nostrils basal, and covered with a shield. Hind toe long, and joined to inner by broad web.

Genus PLOTUS.

πλώς = a swimmer.

Wings long; second and third quills equal and longest. Tail long and broad towards the end, which is rounded. Outer toe as long as the middle one.

1008. Plotus melanogaster. THE INDIAN DARTER.

♂ 32″. Legs black. Bill dusky and yellow. Long and lanceolate scapulars spotted white.—*Female*: Fulvous neck-patch.

Tribe *URINATORES*.

The Auks, Puffins, Guillemots, and Penguins are not represented in India.

The Great Auk (*Alca major*) has the shortest wing of any northern bird, and cannot fly at all.

The Penguins are peculiar to the Southern Seas, and are less capable of flying than the Auks; they move along the ground by trailing on their bellies.

The Razorbill (*Alca torda*), the Common and the Black or Bridle Guillemots (*Uriinæ*), and the Puffins (*Fratercula*) are found in British seas, and a favourite breeding-place is at Handa Island, near Scourie, Sutherland.

GENERAL INDEX.

RASORES. GAME BIRDS. (See page 5.)

Bill strong, short, arched. Wings usually short and rounded. Legs very stout.

FEET FORMED FOR WALKING.

* Not represented in India.

GRALLATORES. SHORE BIRDS. (See page 39.)

Lower part of tibia bare. Tarsus elongated. Wings usually long. Tail usually short. Bill straight or inclining. Outer toe usually joined to middle one by short web and to inner toe occasionally. In a few, toes are bordered by loose web.

ALL FLY WELL, WITH LEGS OUT BEHIND.

* Not represented in India.

NATATORES. WATER BIRDS. (See page 101.)

Legs placed far back. Plumage thick and close, with quantity of down. Hind toe small or wanting. FEET MORE OR LESS FULLY WEBBED.

* Not represented in India.